SEASONAL SPANISH FOOD

SEASONAL SPANISH FOOD

JOSÉ PIZARRO
& VICKY BENNISON

PHOTOGRAPHY BY EMMA LEE
KYLE BOOKS

FOREWORD

Writing the foreword to José Pizarro's marvellous cookbook, I felt on the one hand really pleased to support a colleague who is doing so much to champion Spanish gastronomy and the fantastic products, and on the other hand a huge responsibility for this young chef from Cáceres, so acclaimed in London, England; perhaps I would run the risk of failing to capture, in only a few words, the personality of this great professional of the kitchen? His book is as passionate as it is exciting.

Accepting the challenge with open arms, I acknowledge his great talents. And, thanks to his huge capacity to work hard, tenacity and strength of personality, in less than a decade in London, Pizarro has carved out a name for himself. He has done this, remembering with considerable affection his formative years in Spain, especially working under Julio Reoyo. Already in London by 2004, he had forged an excellent relationship with Brindisa, the most prestigious importer of Spanish produce into Great Britain, which led to a lucky encounter with the founder, Monika Linton. Tapas Brindisa in Borough Market, London was born with Pizarro as partner and head chef. And later on he engaged in new culinary adventures in two further restaurants.

Pizarro shows us undeniably Spanish tapas that always carry his personal trademark. His worship of the most wonderful natural ingredients, especially following the seasons, has also catapulted him to other culinary and professional horizons. He is a great disseminator of the culinary heritage he has learned from his Spanish upbringing and he has worked tirelessly with others to promote the best of Spanish produce.

Seasonal Spanish Food embodies these qualities and Pizarro is more than just a new conquistador (this time culinary); he is the true ambassador of Spain on British soil, with great skill in selecting the very best of seasonal products. The warmth and sensitivity he brings to the recipes he creates shines through on every page.

ELENA ARZAK

Restaurante Arzak
San Sebastián-Donostia
Spain

PARA MIS PADRES

José Pizarro's first head chef job was at El Mesón de Doña Filo, a Michelin-starred restaurant near Madrid in Spain. He then worked as Head Chef at Eyre Brothers restaurant in London and now runs the three hugely popular Brindisa tapas kitchens, named after the Spanish foods import company set up by his colleague Monika Linton. www.josepizarro.com

Vicky Bennison has written books on the food and wines of Andalucía and Mallorca for *The Taste of a Place* culinary guides. This is her first collaboration with José, whom she first met as a regular customer and fan of Tapas Brindisa.

CONTENTS

PIZARRO'S SEASONAL SPANISH FOOD

Home in Spain

I'm back home and I'm enjoying a typical family moment. There's a large plate of homemade, crispy-crusted fish *croquetas* and freshly baked bread on the table. It's dusk. My mother, Isabel, is fretting because Antonio and Cristina, my older brother's eight-year-old twins, haven't appeared, and I'm smiling to myself because I remember when I was their age. I loved to build secret camps with friends in the olive groves above the village, and wouldn't return home until it was too dark to see. The twins are probably with their *amigos* up by the communal washing pools. People don't wash their clothes there any longer, but it's still a great meeting place.

Isabel is more worried about the food than about where her grandchildren are: everyone knows everyone in the village, and everyone keeps an eye on the children, who will eventually scamper home to scolds and hugs. I just love it that the kind of carefree childhood I had still continues.

I grew up in a small agricultural village called Talaván in Extremadura, a rural region of Spain next to Portugal. My family has lived there for generations. One grandfather was the equivalent of the local mayor, and the other ran the bar in the main square.

My dad was a farmer and, although he is now retired, he still takes an active interest in his farm, which he manages with my older brother, Antonio. The farm is on the outskirts of the village, and it's a mix of mostly beef cattle and wheat. There are always some chickens in the farmyard, as well as our own recycling unit in the form of a pig.

When I was growing up, we never had to starve, but as a child I was acutely aware of how people in the recent past had been forced to eat anything and everything, from potato skin peelings to cat or fox meat. This was not unusual; the Spanish had to live through some really tough times politically and economically, and it is still in our memories. It is part of our culture that food is precious and must be respected, and we are incredibly proud of what we produce.

Garden to table

There's a well beneath a walnut tree on our land that fills two terraced pools. It's a great spot in the heat of summer, where frogs plop and bees hum. But, more importantly, these pools are used to irrigate my father Antonio's fruit and vegetable garden, with its mix of citrus and apple trees and year-round supply of vegetables.

Every morning by around seven, he's out in his garden tending the plants. My dad is particularly fond of lettuce and he delights in growing it in time for Christmas.

And so, growing up, the food that appeared on our table was ours, often picked just a couple of hours previously. And we weren't alone: in our village, if a house had a garden it was devoted to growing fruits and vegetables, such as melons, tomatoes, peppers, that kind of thing. Fruit and vegetables not used immediately would be hung from the cool rafters of an outhouse until needed. Freezers and supermarket coolers were unheard of, and cooking in tune with the seasons was just something you did. Actually, it meant that we really savored the food while it was in season: baby artichokes in spring, green beans in summer, squash in autumn, and so on.

So in this book I'm talking about Spanish cuisine from a

family perspective; it's where my feeling for Spanish food comes from, even though I now cook for a living. For me, thanks to my parents, cooking is about putting love on a plate. That might sound a bit sentimental, but it's true.

First steps as a chef

My mother learned most of her recipes from her mother-in-law, my Granny Faustina. Growing up, I used to enjoy watching her bake bread, make a *gazpacho* in summer or an *arroz caldoso* (rice stew) in winter, but I never did any cooking until I left home, at sixteen, to study in Cáceres. I soon realized that if I wanted to eat, I had to cook, and I discovered that I thoroughly enjoyed the process. Meanwhile, I was a terrible student. I preferred parties to studying and it wasn't until I changed courses to catering that I settled down and started working hard.

My first job was in a restaurant in Cáceres. It served traditional food—lots of barbecue and roasts, using local produce. But the main thing that the head chef taught me was discipline and tidiness in the kitchen. It was a great lesson to learn, because my next job was in a hotel restaurant that specialized in weddings and conferences for several hundred guests at a time. I used to get three hours of sleep a night and hardly any vacation—the drop-out rate in this kind of job is huge, but I survived, just barely, and moved to Madrid.

Here, I got the chance to experiment with the fantastic variety of produce Spain has to offer—from the tropical fruit of Andalucía to top-quality fish caught in Galicia. I was given my first head chef job by Julio and Inma Reoyo, owners of El Mesón de Doña Filo, a Michelin-starred restaurant in the mountains outside Madrid. It was a very happy time, meeting other chefs and exchanging ideas. Julio became a mentor and not just a boss; in particular, he encouraged me to experiment with flavors and use the more unusual parts of an animal, such as the cheeks, trotters, and tripe—not all at once, though. One of my favorite recipes from this time is foie gras with lentils, which I still make (see page 197).

London calling

When I first came to London, Spanish food didn't have the cachet of, say, Italian food. I think it's a case of familiarity creating affection—can you imagine your food cupboard without spaghetti? Maybe that's because Italians emigrated in huge numbers all over the world taking their love of pasta, Parmesan, and *la dolce vita* with them. Nowadays, everyone loves Italian food, although I'm not sure that those who stayed at home would necessarily recognize what the rest of the world calls Italian cuisine!

So, why have the wonders and diversity of Spanish cuisine remained a mystery to the British and beyond until recently? Well, Spain was fairly isolated from Europe under General Franco's rule and it

was difficult to emigrate. Then there was the poor reputation of Spanish gastronomy abroad: the only experience that the general public had of Spanish cooking was the frequently horrible food produced for tourists on vacation in the Costa del Sol.

Certainly, when I arrived in the UK, there were very few good restaurants showcasing real Spanish food. Now this has all changed: Spain is confident and culturally cool, and at the same time my customers are more adventurous, wanting vivid tastes and the best ingredients. And that is what we serve in the three Brindisa restaurants.

Tapas Brindisa, next door to London's Borough Market, was the first of the restaurants to open. It was named after the Spanish foods import company, Brindisa, set up 20 years ago by my friend and colleague Monika Linton. She has been a trailblazer, sourcing a range of high-quality foodstuffs from all over Spain to sell both to restaurants and delis, as well as directly to the public through her Borough Market shop. So when she approached me about the possibility of opening a tapas bar, I just couldn't say no.

I'd been working as head chef at Eyre Brothers restaurant in London. David Eyre had revolutionized pub food at The Eagle in Clerkenwell, and he had gone on to open this restaurant in Shoreditch. David is fantastic at producing big gutsy flavors, using lots of fresh herbs such as cilantro and chervil—something we don't use in Spain—and the habit has rubbed off on me. Monika and Tapas Brindisa gave me the chance to produce my own interpretation of Spanish cooking.

Seasons and other inspirations

I always say that my cooking is based on traditional recipes, but given a modern twist. Whenever you read about Spanish cookery traditions, it will always explain the influence of the Phoenicians, Romans, and the 700 years of Arab rule. Actually, I rarely think about this! Coming from Extremadura, I am more aware of the influence of the New World, thanks to several *conquistadores* who were born in the region: Cortéz who conquered Mexico, and Pizarro (no relation) who went off to Peru, to name but two. The culinary riches that these guys brought back included peppers, potatoes, and tomatoes.

It was the monasteries that first became the caretakers of these exotic vegetables. I know this because an hour's drive from my home is the small town of Guadalupe, whose fabulously decorated monastery houses the fabulously dressed Santa María de Guadalupe, or Black Madonna as she is more commonly known. This Virgin Mary draws hordes of pilgrims and the monks here have been growing food to feed the many visitors (as well as themselves) for centuries. The monks still cook today, and I like having lunch there: the food is simple, locally sourced, and seasonal—and somehow I always learn something.

The cornerstone of my cooking is fantastic-quality produce, and I am lucky enough to live and work close to London's Borough Market, where I try to source as many of the ingredients we use in the restaurants as possible. Unlike in supermarkets, the produce at Borough Market varies according to the season: plentiful game and mushrooms in autumn, asparagus in spring, fresh berries in summer—there is always something to look forward to, or discover. I don't think the use of wonderful British fresh meat and vegetables alters the "Spanish-ness" of my cooking.

So, the seasons are the starting point for this book. I am true to my culinary roots, although I think my recipes are fresher and generally have shorter cooking times than my Granny Faustina would approve of.

Cooking complex, innovative—and sometimes slightly crazy—recipes is not my thing, as much as I really admire the creativity of my fellow Spanish chefs who are the alchemists of molecular gastronomy. I think it's good to have all kinds of chefs, and I am one who loves bright flavors, simple techniques, and not too many ingredients. Home cooks can easily make my recipes and that is why I want to share them with you.

SPRING

**Peas * Artichokes * Asparagus * Spinach *
Cheese * Eggs * Salt Cod * Easter * Goat and Lamb * Cocas
and Empanadas * Chocolate and Sweet Pastries**

Despite the countryside being flecked with flowers from January onward, I don't feel as though spring has arrived until I have picked my first wild asparagus. It is a yearly reminder, after the pantry reliance of winter, how food tastes best when it's in season and, better still, freshly picked.

The hens start laying eggs again, right on cue to make delicious *revueltos de asparragos*—scrambled eggs with asparagus. And my dad's vegetable patch starts to produce baby fava beans and artichokes. These, simmered with asparagus and a little onion, make a fantastic vegetable stew. Lent used to mean giving up meat, and it is certainly no hardship with dishes like this.

Fresh goat and sheep cheeses start appearing, and it's a reminder to me, a committed meat-eater, to look forward to goat and lamb; the tender flesh is delicious stewed, roasted, broiled, or even grilled. I can never decide which way I like it best. Well, actually, I can: I like it best when my mother cooks it.

PEA SOUP WITH SERRANO HAM

This is a soup for late spring, when there is still a bit of a chill in the air. It's best made with fresh peas but, since these quickly turn to starch, frozen ones—which keep their sweetness—are a thoroughly acceptable substitute.

Serves 4

8 tablespoons extra virgin
    olive oil
1 shallot, diced
1 garlic clove, finely chopped
1 quart chicken stock
28oz shelled peas
4 thin slices of white bread
    from a small loaf
8 thin slices of Serrano ham
small bunch of mint, leaves
    stripped
salt and freshly ground
    black pepper
extra virgin olive oil,
    for drizzling

Heat 2 tablespoons of the oil in a heavy-bottomed saucepan over medium heat. Sauté the shallot and garlic until soft and golden. Pour in the chicken stock, bring to a boil, and add the peas. Simmer for 4 minutes.

While the stock and peas are simmering, you can start cooking the bread and ham. Heat the remaining oil in a small frying pan until the oil starts to shimmer. Slide the bread, two slices at a time, into the oil and cook until golden on both sides. Remove and place on paper towels to absorb the excess oil. Repeat the process with the ham—you want it crisp and browned. Use more oil if necessary.

Stir the mint leaves into the soup, then use a hand blender to process the mixture to a smooth purée. Season with salt and pepper.

To serve, make four open sandwiches by laying a slice of ham onto each slice of toast. Ladle the soup into warm bowls and then, a bit like launching a paper boat onto a pond, gently float one ham-topped toast in each bowl. Drizzle a little olive oil over each serving.

ARTICHOKES

Artichokes are delicious but a bit laborious to prepare, so if I want to use four in a recipe, I'll prepare twenty and reserve the rest for other recipes. How you go about preparing an artichoke depends on its size and whether a choke (the inedible hairy bit in the middle) has formed.

Golf ball-size artichokes need hardly any work to prepare, as the choke hasn't formed. My favorite way to cook these is to cut the artichokes in half, dip them in batter, and then deep-fry them. Served with aïoli (garlic mayonnaise—see page 140), they taste delicious.

For medium and large artichokes, the first step is to remove the tough outer leaves; keep peeling them off until you reach the pale yellow green leaves beneath. (By the way, if your artichokes are very fresh, you can also eat the stalk just below the flower bud.) Next, slice off the tops of the leaves (roughly the first third), the idea being to expose the tender inner leaves; cut off a bit more if you can't see them. Halve or quarter each artichoke lengthwise. Lastly, use a sturdy teaspoon to scoop out the hairy choke so that you end up with a beautiful artichoke heart.

Once cut, don't let the artichokes sit on the cutting board for long, otherwise they'll start to discolor—put them into a bowl of acidulated cold water while you prepare the rest. I use lemon juice to stop the artichokes from turning black before cooking, but I don't like using lemon juice in the cooking water as I think it affects the flavor of the artichokes. Instead I find other ways to acidulate, by adding tomatoes or wine, for example. And I always prepare and cook my artichokes like the recipe on page 18.

ARTICHOKE AND SHEEP CHEESE SALAD

When I first tried this out with my friend Jonathan at Brindisa, he wanted it put on the menu immediately! If you can, use fresh peas from the garden, otherwise defrost frozen peas in some cold water—but they don't need to be cooked.

Ideally this recipe should use Zamorano, a sheep cheese that has almost the same taste as the better-known Manchego but comes from a different region of Spain, Zamora, which is close to Portugal. If you cannot find Zamorano, Manchego is now fairly easy to find in the US—most supermarkets stock it. Failing that, Parmesan will do.

Serves 4

8 artichokes, prepared
  as recipe on page 18,
  drained from their liquid
4 tablespoons extra virgin
  olive oil
2 tablespoons Moscatel
  white wine vinegar
2 handfuls of arugula
¾ cup shelled peas
¼ cup pine nuts, toasted
3oz Zamorano cheese,
  shaved
salt and freshly
  ground black
  pepper

Prepare the artichokes as the recipe indicates on page 18 for cooked artichokes.

Whisk the oil and vinegar together to make the dressing.

Simply mix the artichokes, arugula, peas, pine nuts, and cheese in a bowl, stir in the dressing, season with salt and pepper, and serve immediately.

COOKED ARTICHOKES

This is the way I always cook artichokes. They can be used in lots of dishes—scrambled eggs, salads, and so on.

Serves about 16
2 tablespoons extra virgin olive oil
1 small onion, diced
1 shallot, diced
2 garlic cloves, sliced
2 ripe tomatoes
¾ cup dry white wine
3½ cups water
20 medium artichokes, prepared (see page 16)

Heat the olive oil in a sauté pan, then cook the onion, shallot, and garlic until soft. Chop the tomatoes and stir the flesh and juices into the onion mixture. Sauté gently until the tomatoes are nicely collapsed—about 10 minutes.

Add the wine and simmer for 4 minutes to evaporate the alcohol. Add the water. Return to a boil and add the artichokes, then simmer for 4 minutes, depending on their size; you want the artichokes to remain crunchy. Remove the artichokes and let them cool. Strain the liquid. Place the artichokes back into the liquid—this mixture will keep for a few days in the fridge.

FAVA BEAN AND ARTICHOKE SAUTÉ

This is an excellent side dish when you have the first of the new season's fava beans, because the baby ones don't have a tough skin. If you use more mature beans for this recipe, boil them first and peel off the skins to reveal the vibrant jade colored slithers. This takes a bit of time, but if you have a sharp, pointy vegetable knife, it won't take too long.

This dish pairs well with fish; try serving it with pan-fried hake, haddock, or cod.

Serves 4
4 large artichokes
1 tablespoon extra virgin olive oil
6oz bacon or pancetta, cubed
1 garlic clove, chopped
2 cups shelled fava beans
salt and freshly ground black pepper
2 mint sprigs, leaves stripped

You want just the artichokes' meaty hearts for this recipe. Cook them as described on the left. When you're ready to cook the dish, simply remove the hearts from the liquid and slice them thinly lengthwise.

Heat the oil over low heat in a frying pan, add the bacon, and cook for a few minutes, until the fat starts to turn golden. Then stir in the garlic, artichokes, and fava beans, season, and continue to sauté the mixture slowly until everything is soft. Sprinkle over the mint leaves and serve at room temperature.

GREEN ASPARAGUS SOUP WITH ROMESCO SAUCE

In Spain, in early spring, town and country folk alike love to forage in the countryside for several different types of wild asparagus (or asparagus-type plants) that twirl up toward the sky. Wild asparagus has an intense flavor and a little goes a long way. For this recipe, in fact, commercially grown asparagus works best.

Romesco sauce, a quintessential Catalan sauce, has many variations but usually includes almonds, hazelnuts, garlic, tomatoes, and, importantly, dried *ñora* peppers. These, or other dried peppers such as *choricero* peppers, are available in speciality markets, but you can also substitute ancho peppers. If you like, you could also add a small slice of a hard sheep cheese, such as Manchego or Zamorano.

Serves 4

romesco sauce

4 large ripe tomatoes
4 tablespoons extra virgin
  olive oil
¼ cup whole blanched
  almonds
¼ cup hazelnuts
1 slice of white bread
2 dried ñora peppers,
  soaked for 2 hours in
  warm water, then drained
2 garlic cloves
1 tablespoon sherry vinegar
salt and freshly ground
  black pepper

soup

2 tablespoons extra virgin
  olive oil
1 shallot, chopped
1 quart chicken stock
2¼lb green asparagus

To make the romesco sauce, first preheat the broiler. Cover a baking sheet with foil (to collect any juices), arrange the tomatoes on top, and broil until the skins are blackened and the flesh cooked. Remove the skins and transfer the tomatoes with any juices to a food processor.

Heat the olive oil in a frying pan over medium to high heat and add the almonds, hazelnuts, and bread. Cook until they are golden brown, then remove from the heat and set aside to cool.

Cut open the soaked peppers and scrape out the flesh with a spoon, then add this to the food processor, along with the garlic, and the bread mixture. Add the sherry vinegar, then pulse the mixture to a chunky paste. Season with salt and pepper. (The romesco will keep for several days in the fridge.)

Now make the soup. Heat the olive oil in a large pan over medium heat and soften the shallot. Add the stock and bring to a boil. Only then add the asparagus; this way you keep the vibrant green color of the vegetable. Cook until the asparagus is tender— this should take around 5 minutes. Cool a little before processing the mixture with a hand blender. Adjust the seasoning as needed.

Ladle out the soup into warmed bowls and add a dollop of romesco sauce before serving.

SPRING VEGETABLE STIR-FRY

This is a supper dish from my childhood; basically, it's a way of using up all the vegetables in your kitchen in late spring, before the tomatoes have ripened. The quantities don't have to be exact, and feel free to substitute or add vegetables according to what you have in your fridge. That's what my mother always did.

Chopped ham or hard-boiled eggs would both be good additions to this dish. You could also try stirring in some salsa verde (see page 95) at the end.

Serves 4
2 medium carrots, cubed
2 medium zucchini, cubed
1 small broccoli head, florets only
1 small cauliflower head, florets only
1 cup fresh green beans, snapped in half
4 tablespoons extra virgin olive oil
2 garlic cloves, chopped
2 thyme sprigs
7oz hard cheese, such as Manchego, grated

Bring a saucepan of salted water to a boil. Since the veggies all cook at different rates, it's best to cook them separately. So, add the carrots and simmer until they are *al dente*. This will take about 5 minutes—it really depends on how big the chunks are. Fish the carrots out with a strainer and repeat with the zucchini and so on, until all the vegetables have been blanched.

Now, heat the oil in a large frying pan or wok over high heat. Sauté the garlic for 30 seconds, then add the vegetables and cook them all until they start to caramelize slightly. The end result should not be a mixture like a ratatouille: the vegetables should still have a slight bite.

Strip the leaves off the thyme and scatter over the veggies. Stir through the cheese then let the mixture cool (to bring out the flavors). Serve with chunks of crusty bread.

CATALAN SPINACH

This typically Catalan combination of ingredients is a perennial favorite of our customers. In Catalonia they like to cook the spinach so that it's completely collapsed and wilted, whereas I prefer it fresh and tossed only briefly in the hot oil. As there is quite a lot of spinach, you can cook it in two batches.

Serves 4
3 tablespoons extra virgin olive oil
1 small shallot, finely diced
¼ cup pine nuts
¼ cup golden raisins
12oz baby spinach leaves
salt and freshly ground black pepper

Heat the olive oil in a large wok. Add the shallot, pine nuts, and raisins and cook until golden.

Add the spinach, and toss the leaves with the other ingredients (as you would a salad). The idea is to warm the spinach through—be careful not to overcook it.

Season to taste with salt and pepper and serve immediately.

SPANISH CHEESES

My dad used to keep a dairy herd, and there would always be a bowl of freshly made unsalted creamy curds in the kitchen for family snacking. Over in Catalonia these are called *mató*, but in our family we simply referred to the curds as *queso fresco*, or fresh cheese. Similar to ricotta, they taste heavenly with honey or, at the other end of the taste spectrum, sprinkled with a little *pimentón de la Vera picante* (hot smoked paprika), extra virgin olive oil, and oregano.

Growing up with cheese helped me to appreciate its complexity and variety. In fact, cheese is a great way to illustrate the uniqueness of local food. Take a simple, easily available ingredient like milk; subject it to varying factors like the time of year, the climate and geography of the region, local traditions, and the temperament of the cheese-maker—and it is magically transformed into something unique. Think of Spanish Manchego and Italian Pecorino—they are both hard sheep's milk cheeses, but taste totally different.

Torta del Casar is a favorite of mine. It is made from the milk of Merino sheep, which are normally farmed only for their wool and meat—the region's arid conditions mean that their milk-producing abilities are limited. Until recently, this oozing farmhouse cheese was produced in such small quantities that it was impossible to buy. Now that there are several cheese-makers producing it, Torta del Casar is easier to find in some regions. A solution made from ground-up wild thistle is used to curdle the milk, then it needs two months' worth of maturing at low temperatures and high humidity to keep the cheese in its semi-solid state. Even today, with the cheese-making process carefully controlled and mechanized, a percentage of the cheeses misbehave: they'll turn solid, or erupt through their rind. I love Torta del Casar: I think its individual, robust character is a true reflection of the Extremadura countryside.

I was also lucky enough to visit Fernando Fregeneda's cheese factory in Zamora recently, where they make Zamorano. Their sheep cheese is made in the simple, old-fashioned way. All that is added to the milk is rennet and then the cheese is washed in a saline solution and dipped in olive oil to produce the rind (this is done a couple of times), and then left to mature for varying degrees of time. I loved the subtle differences between the creamier, younger cheeses and the strong, older ones.

Cheeses are often featured in my recipes, and I'm lucky because Spain produces over a hundred different kinds, ranging from hard spicy cow's milk cheese to soft, fresh goat cheese. Some of them are not easy to find outside Spain, so in the following recipes—and elsewhere in the book—I suggest alternatives that are readily available in most supermarkets.

DEEP-FRIED GOAT CHEESE WITH ORANGE BLOSSOM HONEY

One of my favorite cheeses is the wonderful Monte Enebro goat cheese. I visited an amazing cheese-maker named Raphael Báez and his wife Isabel with my colleague Monika who founded Brindisa. They are a lovely couple, and the love that they have for each other shows in the cheese that they make. Monte Enebro is a log-shaped goat cheese with a soft rind made of a natural yeast mold. Its creamy white interior is rich, a little salty, with a long and complex aftertaste. It's available in some speciality cheese shops, but if you cannot find it, any fresh, firm-textured goat cheese will do.

You might think that deep-frying goat cheese is tricky, but it isn't if you coat it in flour and egg first. In Spain, when you dunk something in flour followed by egg prior to frying it, it's called *a la Romana*. The Italians wouldn't recognize the technique as Roman, but nevermind! It makes either a great appetizer or an unusual dessert.

Serves 4

1 medium raw beet,
  trimmed
extra virgin olive oil,
  for frying
salt
12oz goat cheese, sliced
  into four rounds
½ cup flour
2 large free-range eggs,
  beaten
4 tablespoons orange
  blossom honey

Prepare the beet by slicing it very thinly, ideally with a mandolin. Rinse under cold running water and pat dry.

Pour enough olive oil into a frying pan so that it comes ½in up the sides of the pan. Heat the pan until the oil starts to shimmer. Cook the beet over medium heat until it is crisp. The oil will bubble as the moisture from the beet evaporates, and you'll notice that the bubbles lessen as the beetroot starts changing color. Set aside to drain on paper towels and season with salt.

Next, pat the cheese rounds in flour on both sides so that they are well covered, then dip them in the egg mixture. Pop them into the frying pan two at a time and fry over high heat for about 1 minute—turning the cheese over halfway through—until a golden-brown crust forms. If the cheese is completely covered by the oil, the rounds will only need to cook for 30 seconds. Place the cheese on paper towels to drain.

Arrange the cheese rounds on a flat plate and drizzle the honey over the top in a zig-zag pattern. Serve with the beet crisps.

ANCHOVY AND BLUE CHEESE TOASTS

I first tried this combination of powerful flavors in a tapas bar in central Madrid. It was a mad house, something out of the *Addams Family* or *Cheers*—or a cross between the two. The bartender greeted me with "oh damn, a customer," then he didn't want to serve me any tapas because he had only yesterday's bread. But the staff turned out to be friendly, the bread eventually arrived, and the food was fantastic.

Serves 4

3½oz Picos Blue or a similar blue cheese, such as Stilton
4 slices of good-quality bread
8 anchovy fillets, drained of olive oil
2 mint sprigs, chopped
extra virgin olive oil, to drizzle

Mash the cheese to a paste using a fork. Toast the bread and cut each slice into two triangles. Spread the cheese onto the toast, lay an anchovy on top, then sprinkle with the mint and drizzle with a little olive oil. Eat immediately.

CHICORY AND CABRALES BLUE CHEESE SALAD

Queso Cabrales is a really pungent unpasteurized blue cheese from Asturias, but you could use Gorgonzola or Stilton instead. The bitter taste of chicory combines magically with the strong cheese and fragrant honey to make a refreshing start to a meal. Toasting the walnuts brings out the flavor. This is a great appetizer.

Serves 4

¼ cup walnuts
1 tablespoon orange blossom honey
1 tablespoon Moscatel white wine vinegar
2 tablespoons extra virgin olive oil
3 heads chicory
5¼oz Cabrales blue cheese, cut into ¾in cubes
handful of mixed fresh herbs, such as chervil, mint, and chives
salt and freshly ground black pepper

Preheat the oven to 400°F. Break up the walnuts and put the pieces on a baking sheet to toast in the oven for 4 minutes. They burn very easily, so don't wander off.

Make the vinaigrette: whisk the honey and vinegar vigorously in a small bowl and then slowly add the oil, whisking all the while (this helps the dressing stay as an emulsion).

Separate the chicory leaves, and cut the base of each to a point using a knife.

Arrange the chicory leaves in a flower pattern on a serving plate. Place a cheese cube in the middle of each leaf, then scatter the toasted walnuts over the top, making sure there are several nutty morsels in each "petal." Now pile the herb salad in the middle of the flower and drizzle the dressing over everything. Finish off with a sprinkling of salt and a twist of freshly ground black pepper.

SERRANO HAM AND GOAT CHEESE SALAD

This salad looks great and is very easy to make. The key to its success is using the best ingredients, so try to find high-quality Serrano ham for this recipe; Parma ham would be a good substitute if you cannot find Serrano ham. I like to use Garrotxa goat cheese from Catalonia, but if you cannot find it—or don't like goat cheese—use a sheep's milk cheese like Manchego or even a spicy Cheddar instead.

In Spain, cherries come into season in late spring or early summer, so this salad takes advantage of them. If you cannot find decent cherries, try chopping up some soft, semi-dried apricots instead.

Serves 4

2 cups frisée salad leaves

20 ripe, early season
  cherries, pitted

¼ cup sliced almonds,
  toasted

4 tablespoons extra virgin
  olive oil

2 tablespoons apple
  cider vinegar

salt and freshly ground
  black pepper

7oz Serrano ham, sliced

4½oz goat cheese,
  cut into cubes

8 mint leaves, chopped

Mix the frisée, cherries, and almonds together in a bowl. Whisk together the oil and vinegar, add to the salad, and toss thoroughly. Season to taste with salt and pepper.

Arrange the ham slices around a large plate and heap the salad in the middle. Place the cheese on top of the salad, then scatter the mint leaves over the top and serve.

EGGS

Frying eggs is the easiest thing in the world, but not many people do it well. In Spain, fried eggs are called *huevos con puntilla*—or eggs with a frilly lace hem—and this gives a good clue as to what you're aiming for: crispy edges! There are a couple of important things to remember. The first is to use a small frying pan, about 1½in deep, which you fill to a depth of about ½in with oil. Then, before you add the egg to the pan, heat the oil until it just starts to smoke. Add the egg—it will splutter and sizzle deliciously—and deep fry for 1 or 2 minutes. Use a slotted spoon to scoop out the egg. Lastly, sprinkle some pepper and crunchy sea salt over the top.

ROAST ASPARAGUS WITH FRIED DUCK EGGS AND SERRANO HAM

My parents kept ducks and chickens, and as a child I was always the first to go searching the ducks' nests for eggs to eat. Duck eggs are bigger and richer tasting than chicken eggs. Of course, you can substitute chicken eggs in this recipe—just try to buy free-range and organic. I love this dish with romesco sauce (see page 19).

Serves 4
16 asparagus spears
2 tablespoons olive oil
4 duck eggs
extra virgin olive oil, for frying
salt and freshly ground pepper
5–6oz Serrano ham, thinly sliced

Preheat the oven to 425°F.

Snap any woody stems off the asparagus spears, then coat the spears in the olive oil by pouring a little into your hands and rolling them between your fingers.

Lay the spears in a row on a baking sheet, season them with salt, and roast in the oven for 8 to 10 minutes. Turn them over halfway through cooking. How long you roast them for is dependent on the thickness of the spears, but the leafy tips should have turned a bit crispy.

While the asparagus spears are cooking, fry the duck eggs in hot oil as described on page 30.

Arrange the ham slices on four plates, then place the asparagus spears on top, followed by a fried egg. Grind over some black pepper if you like, then drizzle over a little olive oil to finish. Eat immediately.

SCRAMBLED EGGS WITH GOAT CHEESE AND ASPARAGUS

This is a fantastic brunch dish. I am always experimenting with new ways to serve Monte Enebro goat cheese, and this has become one of my most popular dishes. You can substitute any mild, log-shaped goat cheese, though.

My method of scrambling eggs is easy. First, place a pan over high heat. Then, add olive oil (about 3 tablespoons per 8 eggs) and heat it until it shimmers. At this stage, you can add any non-egg ingredients you want—you are limited only by your imagination, but common Spanish additions are chorizo or blood sausage. Sauté the ingredients until melted or cooked, and only then add the unbeaten eggs and cook over medium heat. Stir slowly and continuously until they are just set.

Serves 4
4 slices of sourdough bread
3 tablespoons extra virgin olive oil
sea salt
16 asparagus spears
2 small garlic cloves, chopped
3½oz mild log-shaped goat cheese
8 large free-range eggs

First, make the toast. Brush the slices of bread with 1 tablespoon of olive oil and grill in a hot, dry pan until lightly browned on both sides. Keep warm while you make the scrambled eggs.

Bring a pan of water to a boil, add a pinch of sea salt, and cook the asparagus for approximately 3 minutes. Drain and cut the stalks into 1in lengths.

Put the remaining 2 tablespoons of olive oil in a non-stick pan and place over medium heat. Add the garlic and cook until it just takes on a light color. Add the cheese and the asparagus. When the cheese starts turning creamy, add the eggs and stir until cooked. Serve on the toast.

POTATO TORTILLA

In Tapas Brindisa we use 33 pounds of potatoes every day for our *tortillas*, or potato omelets. The most important ingredient for a successful potato tortilla is caramelized onions—their sticky sweetness rounds off the flavor of the omelet. Ideally, you need two frying pans to make a tortilla, but you can always wash one up and re-use it.

Serves 4 to 6
7 tablespoons extra virgin olive oil
2 medium white Spanish onions, thinly sliced
salt and freshly ground black pepper
5 medium floury potatoes, such as Russet
6 large free-range eggs, beaten

Heat 6 tablespoons of olive oil in a large non-stick frying pan or wok. Add the onions, season with salt, and cook gently for 20 minutes or so until soft and brown, but not burned.

Peel, halve, and finely slice the potatoes. Add the slices to the onions and cook for 30 minutes over low heat until they are completely cooked. Remove any excess oil with a spoon. Season with salt and pepper. While the mixture is still warm, add the beaten eggs and stir everything well.

Heat the remaining tablespoon of olive oil in a clean, medium (9in diameter is ideal), non-stick frying pan, then add the potato mixture. Stir for 1 minute, then smooth the mixture down and let it cook gently for 10 minutes, until there's a brown crust underneath.

Once the tortilla is cooked on the frying pan side, take a flat plate and place it over the pan. Press the pan and plate together and turn both over together so that the tortilla is now on the plate. Return the pan to the heat, and slide the tortilla back into the pan. It's a bit scary to begin with, but practice makes perfect and it's very easy to get the hang of this technique.

Let the tortilla cool to room temperature before serving. Ideally, leave it for a day before cutting it into wedges.

CHORIZO TORTILLA

Here in London, I belong to The Tortilla Club. Well, it's not a club exactly: we're a group of Spanish and British friends who meet up regularly in a different tapas bar or Spanish restaurant to try out their tortillas. That's our excuse, anyway!

This is a variation on the potato tortilla.

Serves 4 to 6

chorizo mixture
1 tablespoon extra virgin olive oil
1 garlic clove, sliced
1 small red bell pepper, sliced
1 small green bell pepper, sliced
4½oz cured spicy chorizo, diced

tortilla
7 tablespoons extra virgin olive oil
2 medium white Spanish onions, thinly sliced
salt and freshly ground black pepper
5 medium floury potatoes, such as Russet
6 large free-range eggs, beaten

To make the chorizo mixture, simply heat the oil in a frying pan and sauté the garlic, peppers, and chorizo until the peppers have softened and the chorizo has changed color. This will take about 8 minutes. Drain off any excess oil.

Then, follow the same method as for the potato tortilla, but this time stir the chorizo mixture in with the potatoes and onions just before you add the eggs.

I love this tortilla served with aïoli—see page 140.

SPINACH TORTILLA

The key to a lovely, moist spinach tortilla is to use fresh raw spinach.

Serves 4 to 6
5 large free-range eggs
1 medium shallot,
 finely chopped
5oz baby spinach leaves
salt and ground black pepper
2 tablespoons extra virgin
 olive oil

Beat the eggs in a large bowl, then add the shallot and the spinach and mix everything thoroughly. Season with salt and pepper.

Heat the oil in a medium non-stick frying pan, and when it starts to shimmer, pour in the mixture. Cook the tortilla slowly for 10 minutes before flipping the omelet over in the same way as described in the potato tortilla recipe.

SALT COD OR BACALAO

There are almost as many ways to serve *bacalao*, or salt cod, as there are cooks in Spain: stewed, grilled, in salads, or fishcakes: the list is endless. My mother always has some salt cod in the fridge, and my parents eat it at least once a week. Their favorite dish is their *arroz caldoso*, a soupy rice with potatoes, dried peppers, and salt cod.

There are several different grades of salt cod, *bacalao verde* (green salt cod) and *bacalao* (dry salt cod). Green salt cod has white, still-flexible flesh and has to be kept in the fridge. Dry salt cod is a bit grayer and firmer, and it can be kept outside the fridge. Personally I prefer green salt cod.

If you come across bacalao that is as stiff as a board, it is not good quality. You can also tell if bacalao is any good or not from the smell—salty sea aromas are okay, rancid smells are not!

The popularity of salt cod is such that nowadays a lot of it is produced in Norway, Iceland, and Canada, and then exported to Europe and parts of the US. The good news is that you can buy this Arctic Circle bacalao with a clear conscience, as it is produced from sustainable stocks of cod.

To prepare salt cod, tap the excess salt from the fish and place it, skin-side up, in plenty of water in the fridge. Change the water every six hours or so. After 24 hours, the fish should be ready to use. To check if it's "done" or not, take a little piece from the thickest part and taste it—the flesh should not taste salty.

BACALAO WITH MASHED POTATOES AND SPINACH

This delicious combination of salt cod, leeks, spinach, and potatoes was inspired by a dish made by the Guadalupe monastery in Extremadura, although their version is a bit more rustic and heavy. I've separated out the ingredients and put them back together in a cleaner, lighter way.

Serves 4

mashed potatoes

4 garlic cloves

4 tablespoons extra virgin
  olive oil

sea salt

3 large floury potatoes,
  peeled and cubed

2 small leeks, white parts
  only, thinly sliced

bacalao/salt cod

1 tablespoon extra virgin
  olive oil

4 pieces of bacalao/salt cod,
  7oz each (see page 34)

spinach

1 tablespoon extra virgin
  olive oil

7oz fresh spinach, washed

salt and ground black pepper

For the mashed potatoes, peel and slice the garlic cloves lengthwise. Heat the oil in a small frying pan then add the garlic—ideally, the slices should be covered in oil. Cook the garlic over medium heat until it is golden and crisp. The oil will bubble as the moisture from the garlic evaporates, and you'll notice that the bubbles lessen as the garlic starts turning a toasted almond color. Remove the garlic with a slotted spoon and drain on paper towels. Season with salt. Reserve the oil for the mashed potatoes.

Next, cover the potatoes and leeks with salted water to a depth of about 1½in, and boil until both are cooked—about 10 minutes. Drain thoroughly and mash the vegetables, adding the garlicky oil as you do so. Please don't be tempted to use a hand blender, as this will give you a purée that's the consistency of glue. Season to taste, cover, and keep warm while you cook the fish.

Heat 1 tablespoon of olive oil in a large non-stick frying pan until it starts to shimmer. Cook the fish fillets skin-side down for around 3 minutes: you want a beautiful golden crispy skin. Turn the fillets over and cook for 3 minutes longer.

In another frying pan, heat 1 tablespoon of oil and toss the spinach leaves until they have all wilted. Season with salt and pepper.

Divide the mashed potatoes and spinach between four plates, placing them side by side. Arrange a fish fillet on top of both, then decorate with the garlic slices. Drizzle a little olive oil over the top to finish.

SALT COD SALAD

This salt cod salad is called *esqueixada* in Catalan—and it literally means "shredded." I first tasted the dish in Pinotxo, a typical café-cum-bar in La Boquería, Barcelona's famous market. My friends from La Boquería come to London's Borough Market (the two markets are twinned) every year for A Taste of Spain festival—it is great to see my two countries joining together for the festival. There are some great marbled fish counters in La Boquería market, where the staff prepare the salt cod for customers.

You hardly soak the cod at all for this salad, so it is imperative that you use the best-quality fish you can find. The marjoram is my addition; in Catalonia you won't find herbs being used like this. You can eat the salad on its own, or as an accompaniment to grilled fish.

Serves 4

4 (6oz) pieces bacalao/salt cod (see page 34)
½ small red onion, diced
1 scallion, chopped
2 ripe tomatoes, chopped and seeds removed
¼ green bell pepper, diced
¼ red bell pepper, diced
20 black kalamata olives, pitted and chopped
5 tablespoons extra virgin olive oil
freshly ground black pepper
2 marjoram sprigs, leaves stripped

Remove the skin and the bones from the salt cod. Tear the flesh into pieces with your fingers, not a knife; you don't want straight edges, just roughly torn bits. Soak the salt cod in cold water for 40 minutes, changing the water three or four times. You want the fish to still be a bit salty.

Squeeze the salt cod between your hands to remove all the water. Then, to be doubly sure, pat it dry between paper towels.

Mix all the ingredients together, and the salad is ready. That's it—simplicity itself.

If you want to make the salad look even more attractive, use a 4in cookie cutter and fill it with the salt cod. Carefully remove the cutter, sprinkle a few extra marjoram leaves over the top, and finish with a drizzle of olive oil.

EASTER

We Spanish take Easter very seriously indeed, and the solemnity of the processions, vigils, and services during *Semana Santa* (Holy Week) remain an intense thing for me to watch. As an altar boy I was more interested in seeing if I could sneak the odd sip of communion wine rather than my spiritual salvation, but I always behaved myself throughout *Semana Santa*.

Towns everywhere have processions, most of them dating from the 16th century, which start on *Domingo de Ramos* (Palm Sunday), and end on *Lunes de Pascua* (Easter Monday). In Cáceres, where I began my career as a chef, these start with floats depicting Jesus on his donkey and the Virgin Mary in mourning. Hundreds of people, young and old, walk the route several times a day.

This is positively light-hearted in comparison to what goes on in the town of Valverde de la Vera, about an hour's drive northeast from my village, Talaván. On *Jueves Santo* (Holy Thursday), a group called *los empalados*, "the impaled ones," are led through the streets by a lantern-bearer, as they re-enact the road to Calvary. They walk barefoot, with their arms tied tightly to a crossbar and two sharp swords tied to their backs, and wear a crown of thorns.

The Easter Sunday processions are more celebratory. Masses of fresh flowers and palm fronds decorate the floats, there are drums and marching bands, and women wear their *mantillas*. As a student, I'd always visit Trujillo, whose Fiesta del Chiviri is much more my style. My best friends Burgos, Anabel, Consoli, and I used to take to the streets, along with most of the townsfolk dressed in traditional costumes, and sing "*chiviri, chiviri, chiviri*" very loudly, as well as lots of other raucous songs (all penned by a composer who lived in Trujillo several centuries ago). It's a great party atmosphere. Years ago, children used to come with their lambs on Easter Saturday to sell them in the town's main square, to be roasted the following day.

Easter is a quieter occasion in Talaván. As a family, we always make sure we are at home with my parents. And there is, of course, food to be eaten. Good Friday is meatless, so we have a stew of Swiss chard, salt cod, and potatoes. Easter Sunday lunch is a casserole of *cabrito* (kid), followed by *leche frita* (literally "fried milk"). Often the weather is beautiful, so quite a few of our friends venture into the countryside and have a paella picnic. Chocolate Easter eggs don't happen, but we do eat a lot of sweet, honeyed pastries; *torrija*, slices of fried bread flavored with cinnamon, is a popular snack throughout Lent.

KID STEW, MY MOTHER'S WAY

These days, *cabrito*, or kid (young goat) is very difficult to find in my village. My mother has to ask around about a week in advance of when she wants to cook this stew, which she likes to make for a family get-together or celebration. While goat isn't widely eaten in the US, you can try looking for it at your local butcher shop; or, if you live near a big city, check out your local Caribbean market. Failing that, lamb will make a good substitute.

Choricero peppers are medium-size peppers that have an intense, sweet taste; they are always used dry to add flavor to stews or soups. If you cannot find them, use Spanish smoked sweet paprika.

Serves 8 to 10
1 whole kid (approx. 11lb),
   jointed
salt and freshly ground
   black pepper
6 tablespoons extra virgin
   olive oil
4 choricero peppers, or
   1 tablespoon spanish
   smoked paprika (sweet)
4 garlic cloves, peeled
1 bottle (750ml) dry white wine
2 bay leaves

Season the kid with salt and pepper. Heat the oil in a deep, heavy pot over medium to high heat, add the kid and the peppers, and cook until the joints are browned.

Remove the peppers and pound them in a pestle and mortar with the garlic cloves to make a paste. (If you are using paprika instead of the peppers, simply add this to the mortar with the garlic.) Mix the wine with this paste and stir it into the meat.

Add the bay leaves, then cover the pot with a tight-fitting lid and simmer slowly for about 1 hour, until the kid is tender. Add water or more wine from time to time to keep the meat moist.

Serve with a green salad. For my dressing, I always use one part honey, one part Moscatel vinegar, and two parts extra virgin olive oil.

SERVE WITH
A GREEN SALAD

SLOW-ROAST SHOULDER OF LAMB

My good friend Oscar is the owner of Cillar de Silos, a bodega that makes wonderful wines in the Ribera del Duero region of Spain. I like inviting him around for a meal when he visits London because he always brings a fantastic bottle of red, such as his Crianza. To complement the wine, I cook something like this lamb recipe.

The lamb tastes delicious served with a green salad and my baked potatoes and apples.

Serves 4 to 6
1 bone-in shoulder of lamb roast (approx. 5½lb)
8 garlic cloves
handful of flat-leaf parsley leaves
salt and freshly ground black pepper
1 bottle (800ml) dry white wine
¾ cup water
2 tablespoons extra virgin olive oil
3 thyme sprigs, leaves stripped

Trim the lamb of any excess fat or sinew and place it in a large roasting pan.

Using a pestle and mortar, pound the garlic, parsley, and about 1 teaspoon each of salt and pepper to a paste. Pat this mixture all over the lamb roast.

Mix the wine, water, and olive oil together and slowly pour over the lamb while you keep rubbing in the paste. You will end up with a garlicky liquid in the base of the tray. Sprinkle the thyme leaves over the joint. Cover and let the lamb marinate for 2 hours. Preheat the oven to 275°F.

Start cooking the roast with the inner side of the joint facing up: cook for 3 hours, basting the lamb every 15 to 20 minutes. After 3 hours, turn the shoulder over and turn the oven up to 425°F. Roast for another 25 minutes to create a crispy outside. Let it rest for 15 minutes before carving.

BAKED POTATOES AND APPLES

This is a great example of what cooks do when they are faced with a shortage of ingredients—my mother improvised one day and the result became a Pizarro family favorite.

For this dish you should use waxy potatoes because they hold their shape. If you are cooking the potatoes to serve with the shoulder of lamb, you should be able to start them off in the same oven, then simply finish them off while the meat is resting at the end.

Serves 4 to 6
1lb waxy potatoes, peeled and sliced ¼in thick
1lb cooking apples, peeled, cored, and cut into large cubes
1¾ cups onions, sliced
3 garlic cloves, sliced
juice of ½ lemon
½ cup extra virgin olive oil
1 bay leaf
salt and freshly ground black pepper
5 flat-leaf parsley sprigs, chopped

Preheat the oven to 300°F.

Mix all the ingredients (except the parsley) together, place on an oiled baking sheet, and cover with foil. Bake for 10 minutes, remove the foil, then bake for another 15–20 minutes at 425°F, until the potatoes are tender.

Sprinkle with parsley and serve.

BARBECUED LEG OF LAMB

I think recipes for lamb and kid are interchangeable. In Spain, milk-fed lamb is considered the best for eating; I love it, because it brings back happy memories of my childhood. As a chef, though, I have to say that while a still suckling lamb produces meat that is certainly very tender, it lacks the flavor of meat from grazing lambs.

This is a great dish to cook on a grill, and baked potatoes make a delicious accompaniment. You could serve with baby spinach leaves mixed with orange slices.

You can ask your butcher to butterfly the leg, in other words, to bone and then flatten out the meat.

Serves 4
1 leg of lamb (approx. 2lb), boned

marinade
¾ cup pitted kalamata olives
1 (1¾oz) can salted anchovies, including the oil
1 tablespoon capers, rinsed
½ fresh red chile, or to taste
1 large rosemary sprig, leaves stripped
3 tablespoons extra virgin olive oil
freshly ground black pepper

baked potatoes
2lb potatoes, peeled
1 onion, sliced
1 bay leaf
6 tablespoons extra virgin olive oil
salt and freshly ground black pepper

Put all the marinade ingredients in a food processor and pulse the machine on and off to make a paste. Don't add any salt—there is already a lot present. Just add a few grinds of fresh black pepper if you wish.

Cover the meat in the paste and let it marinate in the fridge for a minimum of 12 hours, but ideally 24 hours.

The best way to cook the lamb is on a grill. This is not an exact science, but the way I judge if the coals are hot enough is to place my hand about 8in away from the coals. If I cannot count to four, the coals are too hot. Four seconds is the right heat! Grill for about 10 minutes on each side.

Alternatively, preheat the oven to 425°F and roast the lamb for 20 minutes. Allow the roast to rest for 15 minutes before serving.

For the baked potatoes, preheat the oven to 425°F. Slice the potatoes into ¼in-thick pieces. Mix them with the onion slices, bay leaf, salt and pepper, and enough olive oil to coat everything. Place on a baking sheet, cover with foil, and bake for 10 minutes. After 10 minutes, remove the foil and cook for another 15 or 20 minutes, until the vegetables have turned a nice golden brown.

If you are roasting the lamb in the oven, the potatoes can share the space, although you'll need to allow longer if they are on a low rack; they can be finished off higher up once the meat is resting.

TUNA EMPANADA

My mother always makes tuna empanadas for me whenever I come home. These pastries are made with puff pastry—I recommend you buy it rather than go to the hassle of making it.

Makes 8 pastries

2 tablespoons extra virgin
   olive oil
½ small onion, sliced
1 garlic clove, finely chopped
½ red bell pepper, finely diced
1 ripe and flavorsome
   tomato, chopped
salt and freshly ground
   black pepper
1 (9oz) can tuna in olive oil
2 large free-range eggs,
   hard-boiled and
   chopped small
12oz puff pastry
olive oil, for deep-frying

Heat 2 tablespoons of olive oil in a frying pan and sauté the onion, garlic, and pepper until very soft. Add the chopped tomato, season with salt and pepper, and continue to cook the mixture until the juices have evaporated—about 8 minutes.

Drain the tuna thoroughly and fold it into the mixture. Warm it through and then add the chopped eggs.

Roll out the pastry until it's very thin, around $\frac{1}{16}$in thick, and cut out eight 6in circles. Spoon an eighth of the tuna mixture into one half of each circle, making sure you leave the edges clear. Fold the other half of the pastry circle over the top and stick the edges together with a little water. Finish off by pressing the edges together with the prongs of a fork.

Take a small but deep-sided frying pan and pour in enough olive oil to come roughly halfway up the sides of the pastries. Heat the oil over medium heat until it starts to shimmer but isn't smoking. Fry the pastries one or two at a time, until golden brown. Serve with a green salad.

You can also bake these pastries in the oven at 425°F for about 15 minutes or until golden.

SAVORY COCA

Italians don't have a monopoly on pizzas: the Spanish do them too, only we call them *cocas*. There are some differences, of course: for example, the Italians often add cheese as a topping, while this is not often the case in Catalonia (where cocas come from); the dough base is cut into squares, not rounds or slices; and tomato sauce is never added. Toppings can be sweet or savory, and the variations are almost infinite. I like my cocas to be thin and crispy, and this chicory topping is an unusual alternative to the more traditional spinach and onion mixture.

Serves 4

coca base
1 package instant dried yeast
1½ cups warm water
4 cups bread flour
2 teaspoons salt
2½ tablespoons semolina

topping
1 garlic clove, sliced
6 salted anchovies
4 tablespoons olive oil
4 decent size chicory, sliced
   finely (red ones are pretty)
4 free-range eggs

For the base, dissolve the yeast in the warm water. If you have a food mixer with a dough hook, simply add the ingredients and knead for 4 to 5 minutes until you have soft, slightly sticky dough. Try not to overbeat it. If you are making the dough by hand, sieve the flour and salt into a warm bowl. Make a well in the middle and pour in the yeast mixture. Use a spatula to stir in the flour until a soft dough forms. Then turn it out onto a floured wooden board, cover your hands in flour, and knead the dough gently for about 4 minutes. If you knead the dough too much, it will become springy and more difficult to roll out thinly.

Grease a clean bowl with a little olive oil and transfer the dough to it. Cover with a kitchen towel and let it stand in a draft-free spot until the dough has doubled in size—this should take about an hour.

Preheat the oven to 450°F. Take some parchment paper, cut it into four 16-inch squares, and scatter each with a little semolina—it gives a nice crunchiness to the base. Punch the dough down and divide it into quarters. Take one dough ball and stretch it out with your fingers as thinly as possible on the paper; try and aim for about 1/16in thickness. Don't worry about the shape—square or round—but avoid a "high rise" ridge around the edges. Repeat with the other dough balls.

Slip the coca base, still on its sheet of paper, onto a flat baking sheet and put it into the oven. You will probably have to do the cocas in two batches. Bake for about 10 minutes.

While the cocas are baking, make the topping. Crush the garlic and anchovies together and then stir in the olive oil. Toss the chicory in the anchovy dressing. Once the 10 minutes are up, remove the cocas and scatter the chicory mixture over the top. Return to the oven for another 5 minutes, until the chicory leaves start to turn color.

Meanwhile, poach the eggs until the whites are cooked and the yolks are only just starting to set. Coarsely chop the eggs together. Scatter the eggs over the cocas and eat immediately.

DIONI'S PASTRY CAKE

My great friend Dioni is a very good cook, who has gained something of a reputation for herself as a caterer. She was thrilled when a local television station asked her to demonstrate this recipe, which as far as I know is special to my region of Extremadura. Dioni assesses quantities by eye and uses half an eggshell to measure out her vinegar. According to her, this cake is suitable for all kinds of celebrations.

Serves 4

6 large free-range eggs,
   beaten
1 cup extra virgin olive oil
2 tablespoons sherry vinegar
6 cups all-purpose flour
plenty of olive oil, for frying
2 cups honey
3 tablespoons toasted
   slivered almonds

Mix the eggs, oil, and vinegar in a bowl, then slowly beat in the flour. You should end up with a pliable but firm dough. Roll the dough out onto a floured surface. Break off pieces of dough and roll them into "breadsticks" about the thickness and length of a pencil.

Add enough olive oil to cover the bottom of a non-stick frying pan to a depth of about ¾in, and heat it until hot but not smoking. Fry the pastry sticks until they are golden on all sides: you will need to do this in batches. Once cooked, pop them onto paper towels to drain. Break the pastry sticks into ¾in lengths.

Heat the honey in a large saucepan over medium heat until it is hot and liquid, then fold the pastry sticks in carefully. Keep stirring the honey and pastry mixture until the honey turns pale brown. Take a flat serving platter or baking tray and cover it with parchment paper. Place a small glass bowl upside down on the platter and then turn out the mixture around the bowl. Next, wet your hands and shape the mixture into a doughnut shape while it is still warm. Sprinkle the cake with the toasted slivered almonds.

Let cool. Just before serving, remove the glass bowl.

CHOCOLATE TOAST

The Spanish equivalent of Nutella is called
Nocilla. My routine after school was to go home
via my grandmother Gregoria, who would make
me chocolate spread toast. This is the grown-
up equivalent, developed with my friend Enric
Rovira—a well-known chocolatier in Spain.

The salt and floral extra virgin olive oil bring
out the flavor of the plain chocolate. Try to use
top-quality extra virgin olive oil, such as an
Arbequina from Catalonia, and dark chocolate
that contains at least 70 percent cocoa solids;
make sure you choose a thin not chunky bar,
because you want the chocolate to melt quickly.
We made it with Enric's beautiful dark chocolate,
which has a pattern on it that replicates the street
tiles used to pave the sidewalks in Barcelona.

This goes wonderfully with orange sorbet
(see page 216).

Serves 4

4 thin slices of good-quality white bread
16 squares of plain chocolate (70% cocoa solids)
½ teaspoon sea salt
1 teaspoon top-quality extra virgin olive oil

Preheat the oven to 350°F.

Toast the bread. Arrange four squares of
chocolate on each slice, place on a baking tray,
and bake for 30 seconds, until the chocolate
starts to melt.

Remove, and sprinkle with a few crystals of sea
salt and some drops of olive oil.

FRIED CUSTARD

Leche frita translates as "fried milk," but actually it's
a kind of sweet custard fritter, a dish to eat at the end
of a meal or with tea or coffee. It is a dish that is very
close to my heart, as my mother makes it whenever
there is something to celebrate or friends have
dropped in for a visit.

Serves 4 to 6
custard
1 quart whole milk
peel of ½ orange
peel of ½ lemon
1 cinnamon stick
½ cup flour
⅔ cup cornstarch
⅔ cup superfine sugar
4 large free-range
  egg yolks

to coat and fry
1 cup all-purpose flour
2 free-range eggs,
  beaten
⅔ cup extra virgin
  olive oil

½ cup superfine sugar
1 teaspoon ground
  cinnamon, or to taste

Heat the milk, both peels, and the cinnamon in a
non-stick saucepan until very hot, but not boiling.
Leave to infuse for about 30 minutes. Turn off the
heat and remove the cinnamon stick.

Beat the flours, sugar, and egg yolks together
in a bowl. Gradually add the hot milk, beating
continuously. Once you have a thick sauce, scrape
this back into the saucepan and place it over
medium heat to cook for 10 minutes. Stir regularly.
You will end up with a very thick custard. Use a
spatula to smooth the custard onto a baking sheet
to a thickness of ¾in. Let cool in the fridge.

Put the flour and eggs in separate bowls. Cut the
custard into 1in squares and roll each cube in the
flour, then dunk it in the egg. Heat enough oil in
a heavy frying pan to submerge the custard cubes.
Once the oil starts to shimmer, cook the squares in
batches for 1 minute until pale golden, and drain
on paper towels. Mix the sugar and cinnamon
together and dust them thoroughly.

TOCINO DE CIELO

"Heavenly bacon" is an odd name for a dessert, but the nickname probably stems from the custard tart's vague resemblance to bacon. Every book on Spanish cooking has a recipe for this dish: it's a classic, and I make no apology for including it in this book. The tart can be very sweet, so I like to serve it with berries to balance the flavors.

Serves 4

caramel
½ cup superfine sugar
3 tablespoons water
3 drops lemon juice

custard
1 vanilla pod
1⅓ cups superfine sugar
1 cup water
6 large free-range egg yolks
1 large free-range egg

¾ cup raspberries
¾ cup redcurrants

Preheat the oven to 300°F.

First, make the caramel. Put the superfine sugar, water, and lemon juice in a small saucepan, bring to a boil, then simmer until the liquid turns nut brown; this will take about 10 minutes. Pour the caramel into a 9in-round cake pan, carefully tilting the pan so that the bottom is completely covered. Set aside to cool.

To make the *tocino*, first split the vanilla pod lengthwise, remove the seeds, and add these, along with the sugar and water, to a pan. Bring slowly to a boil and simmer gently to make a syrup. To check if the syrup is done, take a teaspoon of the liquid and test it between your finger and thumb; it is ready when a strand of syrup appears as you move your fingers slowly apart.

Beat the egg yolks and whole egg together in a bowl. Slowly drizzle the syrup into the mixture, beating all the time. Try not to create any foam.

Sieve the egg mixture into the cake pan. Place the pan in a *bain marie* (a deeper pan with water in it halfway up the sides) and bake for 20 minutes—the custard should be firm. Let cool, then place in the fridge.

Turn the *tocino* out onto a plate. The way to do this is to put the plate on top of the pan and, pressing the two together, turn it upside down. It just takes courage. Mix the raspberries and redcurrants together, cut up the *tocino*, arrange the slices with the fruit on four plates, and serve.

CHOCOLATE CAKES WITH CHOCOLATE PAPRIKA SAUCE

The Spanish love chocolate, particularly "drinking chocolate," which you buy as a bar to melt. The smokiness of smoked paprika, or *pimentón*, does wonders with chocolate—but you cannot cook the two together, because the paprika will turn bitter. The way around this problem is to make a sauce, and stir in the spice at the last minute. This recipe was developed by my good friend Vicky.

You can use ramekins for this recipe, but the soufflés are easier to remove if you use muffin tins with straight sides and removable bottoms.

Serves 6

cakes
7oz plain chocolate (70%
  cocoa solids), chopped
1 stick salted butter, cut into
  ½in cubes
6 large free-range egg yolks
½ cup superfine sugar
2 large free-range egg whites

chocolate paprika sauce
3.5oz chocolate (70% cocoa
  solids)
3 tablespoons extra virgin
  olive oil
⅓ teaspoon spanish smoked
  paprika (mild)

handful of cherries

Preheat the oven to 400°F. Butter six 1-cup muffin tins or ramekins and arrange on a baking sheet.

Place the chocolate and butter in a heavy, medium-size saucepan and stir over low heat until melted and smooth. Don't let the mixture boil. Remove the pan from the heat and let the sauce cool to lukewarm, stirring occasionally.

Meanwhile, use an electric hand whisk to beat the egg yolks and all but 1 tablespoon of the sugar in a large bowl, until the mixture is thick and pale; this will take about 5 minutes. Fold a tablespoon of the egg mixture into the melted chocolate, then fold this back into the remaining egg mixture in the bowl.

In another bowl, beat the egg whites until soft peaks form. Add the remaining tablespoon of sugar and continue to beat the whites until you have created stiff peaks. Using a metal spoon, fold the egg whites into the chocolate mixture, then divide this equally between the muffin tins or ramekins.

These little cakes are nice still a little gooey in the middle, so bake them until the edges are set but the centers still soft, which takes about 12 minutes. Cook for a couple of minutes longer if you want a firm middle. Remove the tins from the baking sheet and cool for a couple of minutes.

To make the sauce, melt the chocolate with the olive oil, stirring regularly. Keep warm and, just before serving, stir in the paprika.

To serve: slide a knife around the sides of the tins to loosen the cakes if necessary. Slip the cakes out of the tins and arrange on plates. Drizzle a little sauce over each. Serve with some cherries, and eat while still warm.

SUMMER

**Tomatoes ✳ Zucchini ✳ Melon ✳ Vinegar ✳ Beans ✳
Beets ✳ Peppers ✳ Fresh Fish ✳ Tapas ✳ Summer Fruits**

Summer for me means vacation. And vacations mean barbecues by the beach, bright salads—and staying up until three in the morning.

It is the time of year when my dad's garden produces more vegetables than we can eat. Large ribbed tomatoes, sweet cherry ones, all sun-ripened and intensely flavored. Several varieties of lettuce have to be harvested every day, partly to stop the rabbits, and we have the pleasure of picking zucchini when they are no bigger than a thumb. He grows lots of herbs too, but he thinks parsley should be cooked and is horrified when I put it into salads to eat raw.

I think vinegar is one of the more underrated ingredients in the kitchen.

I use various types of vinegar all year round, but it comes into its own in summer. Vinegar preserves food, heightens flavors, and refreshes one's palate—a good thing when the fierce heat dulls everyone's appetites.

Summer also means fresh fruit. There would be no problem in getting people to eat their five portions of fruit and vegetables a day if the fruit sold in supermarkets was properly ripe. If you ever get a chance to pick a peach or nectarine straight from a tree and suck on its delicious juices, do it! You'll know what ripeness means. Fruit like this doesn't need any help or disguise, so do what the Spanish do and finish a meal with a bowl of strawberries, cherries, or whatever is perfectly in season.

TOMATO JAM

Like everyone else in rural Spain, we always grow enough tomatoes to bottle as a sauce for the winter months. Aside from its obvious use in casseroles and soups, the sauce is fantastic spread on toast for breakfast. This recipe for tomato jam is also a great accompaniment to a variety of cheeses.

Makes approx. 1¼ cups
2lb ripe tomatoes
½ cup superfine sugar
½ cup demerara sugar
1 cinnamon stick
peel of ½ lemon
peel of ½ orange

Use a sharp knife to make a cross in the skin of the base of each tomato. Bring a saucepan of water to a boil. Add the tomatoes and simmer for 2–3 minutes.

Use a slotted spoon to remove the tomatoes from the pan and plunge them into iced water. Remove the skins and the stem. Chop the tomatoes into 6 to 8 slices, reserving the juice.

Place the tomatoes and juice in a saucepan over low heat and let reduce for 10 to 15 minutes, until most of the water has evaporated. Now add the rest of the ingredients and give everything a good stir. Don't break up the cinnamon.

Slowly cook the tomatoes for about 1 hour, stirring regularly. The end result should be a sticky, firm jam that is a shiny brown-red color. Remember to remove the cinnamon stick.

This keeps well in the fridge.

TOMATO SALAD WITH SMOKED PAPRIKA

The first time my dad came to London, we visited Borough Market, where we bought some cherry tomatoes—something that we don't have in our area. He took the tomatoes home and grew his own plants from the dried seeds. Now they are an annual feature in his vegetable garden. The best time to pick tomatoes is early in the morning, when they still smell earthy sweet.

This salad is great with grilled fish. I like to use different colored tomatoes, which look very pretty and, of course, taste amazing.

Serves 4
1lb tomatoes, ripe but not soft
1 garlic clove, finely chopped
½ red onion, finely sliced
1 teaspoon spanish smoked paprika (bittersweet)
4 tablespoons extra virgin olive oil
2 tablespoons Cabernet red wine vinegar
salt and freshly ground black pepper
1 oregano sprig, leaves stripped

Slice the tomatoes and arrange the pieces artistically on a plate. Sprinkle the garlic and red onion over the tomatoes, followed by the paprika. Whisk together the oil and vinegar and pour this, the dressing, over the tomatoes. Finish off with some salt and pepper and a scattering of oregano leaves. Let sit for 5 minutes to let the flavors develop before serving.

GAZPACHO

In my family there is always a pot of gazpacho in the fridge during the summer months. When it's 100°F outside, there is nothing more refreshing than a gulp of this cold soup. It is my nephew Antonio's favorite soup. He likes to help make it, acting as a self-appointed quality controller who has to taste everything from the picked tomatoes to the end result.

Naturally, good-quality and flavorful ingredients are essential.

Serves 4
2lb ripe tomatoes
2 scallions, sliced
¼ small cucumber, coarsely chopped
½ garlic clove
approx. 1 tablespoon sherry vinegar
5 tablespoons extra virgin olive oil
salt and freshly ground black pepper

This soup is just so easy: essentially, you're aiming to make an emulsion. Simply put all the vegetables and the vinegar into a food processor. Then, with the motor running, slowly add the oil through the funnel. If the soup is too thick, add a little water to thin it out. Chill for 4 hours.

Just before serving, add salt and pepper and adjust the vinegar balance if necessary.

MELON GAZPACHO

We're all familiar with the classic gazpacho made with tomato and cucumber, but in Spain the name covers lots of different chilled bread soups, all of them delicious. In my area of Extremadura, for example, we have our own version known as *gazpacho extremeño* or *en trozos*, which means "in pieces": the ingredients are chopped up rather than blended in a processor, resulting in a chunky rather than smooth soup. All sorts of ingredients are used, too. People make a partridge gazpacho; an herb gazpacho, made with an intense-tasting plant called *poleo*, which is a cross between mint and thyme that grows everywhere in the heat-baked countryside; and this, a particular favorite of my mother's, made with melon. It's a fabulously refreshing soup, and isn't so unusual when you remember that tomatoes are fruit, too.

When making a chunky rather than a smooth gazpacho, it's even more important than usual to use the most flavorsome ingredients you can get ahold of.

Serves 4
½ small, mild white onion, finely diced
2 beefsteak tomatoes, seeded and diced
1 small melon, seeded and diced
1 large green bell pepper, seeded and diced
1 tablespoon superfine sugar
5 tablespoons extra virgin olive oil
3 tablespoons sherry vinegar
1 quart water
4 slices white bread, in chunks
salt and freshly ground black pepper

Simply mix all the ingredients together in a bowl, cover, and chill for at least 4 hours before serving.

GAZPACHO VERDE

My family can now drive from Extremadura to Cádiz for our annual seaside vacation in three hours, thanks to a new roadway. We pass through the Sierra Morena where a green, herby variant of gazpacho is popular. Fresh cilantro is often featured in Portuguese cooking, and I suspect its use has spread over the border— culinary traditions are not respectful of lines on a map! This recipe is one that my sister Isabel, who is a great cook, gave to me.

Serves 4
large bunch of fresh cilantro, leaves only
1 slice of white bread
1 small garlic clove
1 cucumber, about 8in, coarsely chopped
5 tablespoons extra virgin olive oil
2 tablespoons sherry vinegar
3¼ cups water
salt and freshly ground black pepper
4 hard-boiled eggs, chopped
2 medium Gem lettuces, sliced
¼ cup flaked almonds

Place the cilantro, bread, garlic, and cucumber in a food processor and pulse the ingredients to a paste. Set aside to marinate for 1 hour. Stir in the oil and vinegar, followed by the water. Season with salt and pepper. Chill in the fridge for a couple of hours.

Divide the eggs and lettuce between four bowls and pour in the gazpacho. Scatter the almonds over the top of each serving.

ZUCCHINI SALAD

This is a great side salad best made with home-grown zucchini that are bursting with flavor— not the hydroponically grown ones sold when these vegetables are naturally out of season.

Serves 4
4 medium zucchini
3 tablespoons extra virgin olive oil
salt and freshly ground black pepper

dressing
5 tablespoons extra virgin olive oil
3 tablespoons Moscatel white wine vinegar
salt and freshly ground black pepper
1 small shallot, very finely diced
small handful each of flat-leaf parsley and
   cilantro, finely chopped
1 large free-range egg, hard-boiled and
   finely chopped

Heat a ridged cast-iron grill pan or a heavy frying pan until sizzling hot.

Cut the zucchini into strips about ½in thick. Mix the slices with the olive oil and salt and pepper in a bowl and let sit for 5 minutes. This will help the zucchini caramelize. Place the strips in the pan in one layer. Grill for about 2 minutes, brush the tops with oil, then use tongs to flip the slices over. Cook for another minute or so. The zucchini should be lightly caramelized and golden, not burned. Arrange the slices on a plate.

Whisk together the olive oil, vinegar, and salt and pepper in a small bowl. Stir in the shallot, parsley, and chopped egg. Dot and smear this dressing over the zucchini slices, making sure none miss out on their benediction.

Let sit for 30 minutes or so for the flavors to get to know each other.

ALMOND SOUP WITH MELON

In my village, the most commonly planted melon is the Kharbouza, which has the nickname *piel de lagarto*, or "skin of a lizard." Its sweet crunchiness makes it a good companion to this popular garlicky almond soup, known as *ajo blanco* ("white garlic") in Spain. Of course, feel free to use other kinds of melon, such as Cantaloupe or Honeydew. For a variation, you can substitute the melon for cherries and add one dessert apple.

Serves 4

2 to 3 pieces crustless, day-old white bread, torn

3¼ cups water

2 cups blanched whole almonds

1 garlic clove, chopped

¾ cup extra virgin olive oil

3 tablespoons sherry vinegar, or to taste

sea salt

¼ melon, seeded and cubed

Soak the bread in the water for about 15 minutes until the pieces are soggy. Then put the softened bread and the water in a food processor with the almonds, garlic, and olive oil and process, pulsing the machine on and off, until smooth. Season to taste with sherry vinegar and sea salt. Transfer to a lidded container and refrigerate until the soup is well chilled; this will take 2 to 3 hours. Chill the melon cubes at the same time.

Give the soup a stir and adjust the seasoning if necessary. Ladle into soup bowls and divide the melon cubes between them. Drizzle with a little olive oil.

ZUCCHINI SOUP WITH CHEESE

This is a soup my mother is fond of making when there's a glut of medium-size, still-flavorful zucchini. She likes to use Dairylea cheese to make the soup creamy, because the local goat and sheep cheeses have too strong a taste. I like to use cream cheese.

Serves 4

2 tablespoons extra virgin olive oil, plus extra for drizzling
1 garlic clove, chopped
1 shallot, chopped
3 medium zucchini, coarsely cubed
salt and freshly ground black pepper
1 quart chicken stock
7oz cream cheese
shaved Zamorano or Parmesan
3 flat-leaf parsley sprigs, chopped

Heat the oil in a frying pan over medium heat and soften the garlic and shallot until they are translucent in color. Add the cubed zucchini, season with a pinch of salt, and continue to cook the mixture for about 5 minutes.

Add the stock and simmer for about 10 minutes until the zucchini is completely cooked. Now add the cream cheese and use a hand blender to purée the soup—you want it thick and creamy. Adjust the seasoning.

Divide the soup between four warmed bowls, then scatter the cheese and parsley over, drizzle a little olive oil over each, and serve immediately.

VINEGAR

I have a hunch that lots of people think vinegar is just vinegar, and that's part of the reason why there are so many pre-prepared dressings on the supermarket shelves. But nothing could be further from the truth.

If you think about it, we all know the importance of a good extra virgin olive oil when it comes to making a dressing—how it can enhance the flavors of a dish if you drizzle some over the top just as you serve it. Good vinegar does the same thing, although of course its acidity tickles the taste buds in an entirely different way. It accentuates and lifts the other flavors in a dish, without overwhelming them.

You've probably already discovered that if you leave an opened bottle of wine on your counter for a week or so, the wine doesn't automatically turn into vinegar; it needs special bacteria called acetobacters. What is more, even if you have the right microbes, you cannot make good vinegar from poor-quality wine, and you certainly cannot make it in a hurry. So, it's hardly surprising that you will have to pay a bit more for something that has a well-rounded flavor, rather than

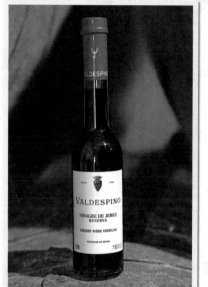

a sharp, tooth enamel-destroying taste. But, trust me, it's well worth hunting out decent vinegars from your local supermarket.

I love using vinegar in my cooking—and I'm lucky because there are some exceptional Spanish wine and sherry vinegars to choose from, each with their own particular taste and pungency. Here are some of my favorites.

Moscatel wine vinegar
The sweetness of this vinegar is due to the high sugar levels present in the original Moscatel wine, which give it a lovely honeyed, but tangy, taste. I use Moscatel vinegar a lot. I make countless salad dressings with it, and I find its subtle flavors are wonderful in fish salads. It also pairs very well with fruit desserts. If you have trouble finding stores that stock it, then use a good-quality white wine vinegar and add a touch of honey.

Vinagre de Jerez
I really like sherry vinegar, which is produced by the same *solera* method used to make sherry: older vinegars are gradually mixed with newer ones and kept in oak barrels (originally used for making sherry) for 8 to 10 years. The result has a sweet, smooth, and complex flavor that works beautifully

with garlicky dishes and gutsy vegetable combinations such as gazpacho. It is wonderful for perking up lentils, too, although I find that it's too strong for white fish and green salads.

My friends think I'm crazy, but a few drops scattered over a fried egg is my standby whenever hunger strikes—I mop up the sticky yolky-vinegar juices with a big chunk of bread. Delicious!

Cabernet red wine vinegar

This is another vinegar I use regularly. As you'd expect, it has a more robust taste than the Moscatel and I find it happily zings up the flavors in tomato salads, grilled sardines, and goat cheese.

PX sherry vinegar

The Pedro Ximénez grape results in very dark, sweet, and sticky wines and sherries, which, like sherry vinegars, are produced using the *solera* method. You can see how the color of the vinegar changes as it matures in the picture below, left. The vinegar retains the raisiny, figgy fruit flavors of the wine and it's good in both savory and sweet dishes. I like it best boiled down to make a syrup—called a reduction—which I serve with pan-fried foie gras. The tangy sweetness contrasts nicely with the rich subtle-tasting liver. Aged PX sherry vinegar, which has simply spent longer in the barrels, has a greater viscosity, sweetness, and depth of flavor. Italy's balsamic vinegar from Modena makes a reasonable substitute.

There are loads of other vinegars, and it's fun to experiment. But remember that vinegars have varying levels of acidity, so be cautious and add only a few drops at a time.

GREEN BEAN SALAD WITH ANCHOVIES

This salad is similar to France's *salade niçoise*—but I've given it my own Spanish twist by omitting the tuna and not mixing up the ingredients too much.

Serves 4

4 large free-range eggs, at
    room temperature
7oz fresh green beans
12 anchovy fillets in olive oil
3½ tablespoons salted
    capers, rinsed
20 Kalamata black
    olives, pitted
16 cherry tomatoes
4 tablespoons extra virgin
    olive oil
2 tablespoons Cabernet
    red wine vinegar
salt and freshly ground
    black pepper

Bring a saucepan of water to a vigorous boil. Add 1 teaspoon of salt, then lower the eggs into the pan and boil for 6 minutes: you want eggs with a runny yolk but firm white. Carefully remove the eggs from the boiling water and immediately plunge them into iced water. This stops the eggs from cooking and makes them easy to peel.

Next, in another saucepan of fresh, boiling water, simmer the beans for 3 minutes, so that they are cooked but retain some crunch. Drain and refresh the beans under running cold water.

Place the anchovies, capers, olives, and tomatoes in a bowl, give it a good stir, and set aside.

Make the vinaigrette by whisking the oil and vinegar together, then pour it all over the salad. Season to taste with salt and pepper, but be careful with the salt; there are quite a few salty ingredients already in the salad.

Divide the salad between four plates or place on one serving dish. Cut the boiled eggs in half and place sunny-side up on top of the salad.

GREEN BEANS WITH SERRANO HAM AND POACHED EGG

My dad loves his green beans boiled for half an hour—he says mine are undercooked—and then sautéed with garlic. We use the flat green beans (sometimes called Italian flat beans in the US) rather than the rounded or French green bean. When they are less than 4in long, they have the texture of silk.

Serves 4

2¼ cups green beans, ends trimmed

3 tablespoons extra virgin olive oil

2 small garlic cloves, chopped

salt and freshly ground black pepper

7oz Serrano ham, diced

4 large free-range eggs

½ teaspoon white wine vinegar

Bring plenty of salted water to a boil in a saucepan, add the beans, and cook for 3 minutes, until they are *al dente*. Drain, then plunge the beans into iced water to cool them and keep them a lovely green color.

Heat the oil in a frying pan and sauté the garlic until it starts to change color. Add the beans and season with salt and pepper if you wish—although you shouldn't need to since the beans were cooked in salted water and you're going to add the salt-rich ham. Sauté for an extra minute, add the ham, and give everything a good stir.

Meanwhile, bring a pan of water to a gentle simmer. Add the vinegar and a pinch of salt. Crack the eggs into a ramekin and slide them one at a time into the water. Cook for about 4 minutes. Scoop out the eggs and drain them on paper towels.

Divide the bean and ham mixture between four plates, then slide an egg on top of each serving. To eat this, attack the egg with a knife and fork: you want the creamy yolk and chopped-up white mixed through the beans.

BEET AND GOAT CHEESE SALAD

This is an unlikely combination of ingredients, but it works really well and looks pretty too. We use Monte Enebro cheese (see page 25), but any semi-cured log-shaped goat cheese that's soft with a bit of a rind makes a good substitute. Just make sure you choose one that keeps its shape when it's cut up into cubes.

I find a mandolin useful for this recipe, because I like the beets and onion sliced whole to produce lovely purple and magenta circles.

Serves 4

dressing
1 cup shelled walnuts
6 tablespoons extra virgin
   olive oil
2 tablespoons Moscatel
   white wine vinegar
salt and freshly ground
   black pepper

beet salad
8 raw small beets
½ red onion, peeled
   and left whole
9oz semi-cured goat
   cheese, cubed

4 mint sprigs, leaves
   stripped and torn

Preheat the oven to 425°F. Break the walnuts into pieces (but not too small), and spread them on a baking sheet. Place in the oven for 4 to 6 minutes—the nuts will start to turn color and smell toasty. Remove and let them cool. Remove any debris such as skin and small bits of nut.

Whisk the oil and vinegar together and add a pinch of salt and pepper. Stir in the walnuts and set to one side.

Next, cook the beets. You can either bake them in the oven or boil them. I find the latter is less hassle: simply put the beets in cold unsalted water, bring to a boil, and simmer for around 25 minutes. The vegetables should still have a bit of crunch in the middle. Drain, rinse in cold water, and set aside to cool. Peel and slice the whole beets into circles roughly ¼in thick and season. Using a mandolin or a very sharp knife, slice the onion as thinly as possible.

Place the beet layers on four plates and then the cheese and onion. Drizzle with the walnut vinaigrette, season again to taste, sprinkle the mint leaves over the top, and serve immediately.

SAUTÉED BEETS

This simple dish is excellent with grilled fish such as mackerel.

Serves 4
14 small raw beets, skin on
3 tablespoons extra virgin olive oil
1 garlic clove, chopped
salt and freshly ground black pepper
5 tablespoons Cabernet red
  wine vinegar
2 tarragon sprigs, leaves stripped

Place the beets in cold, unsalted water. Bring to a boil and simmer for about 20 minutes. The vegetables should still have a bit of crunch in the middle. Drain, rinse in cold water, and let cool. Peel and slice them into ½in thick wedges.

   Heat the oil in a frying pan and sauté the garlic; as it starts to color, add the beets and cook for another minute. Season with salt and pepper, then add the vinegar and tarragon leaves. Reduce the vinegar until it has almost disappeared; this will take about 4 minutes. Don't hurry: keep the heat low, otherwise the vinegar will burn and taste horrible. The end result is a lovely, glistening mound of beets.

PADRÓN PEPPERS

This classic tapas is popular all over Spain, although both the dish and the peppers originate from the Padrón area of Galicia. Padrón peppers are small, green, and mild. Well, mostly… every so often you find one that's fiery-hot, so eating a plate of these can be a bit like playing Russian roulette.

   The most difficult part of this recipe is finding the Padrón peppers in the first place. Some speciality stores stock them, as well as larger supermarket branches. Failing that, they are very easy to grow, and incredibly addictive to eat.

Serves 4
3 tablespoons extra virgin olive oil
7oz whole Padrón peppers
sea salt flakes

Heat the oil in a frying pan, then add the peppers in a single layer. Keep moving them as they fry. It is important not to overcook the peppers: as soon as the skin starts to turn brown and blister, place them on a plate covered with paper towels. Once drained, transfer them to a serving plate and sprinkle generously with salt flakes. Eat immediately.

GRILLED PEPPER AND CURD CHEESE SALAD

Ensalada zorongollo comes from the region of La Vera in the north of Extremadura, famous for growing peppers. It's not surprising that the folks there have developed a variety of pepper salads, and this is one example. I first came across it just after I'd passed my driving test and I toured La Vera with friends. I had to sleep in my car; I've still got the car and it brings back many happy memories.

The mix of grilled peppers and fresh cheese is just gorgeous. In the US, there is no direct equivalent of Spain's fresh curd cheeses, such as Catalonia's *mató*. If you can't find any in a speciality store, mozzarella is a good substitute.

Serves 4 to 6
4 red bell peppers
4 large ripe tomatoes
salt and freshly ground black pepper
6 tablespoons extra virgin olive oil
12 salted anchovy fillets, drained
10½oz fresh curd cheese or
   mozzarella, sliced
3 oregano sprigs, leaves stripped and chopped

Place the peppers and tomatoes under a preheated broiler until the skins are blackened. Remove, place in a bowl, and cover with plastic wrap for 5 minutes. Peel off their skins and slice.

Season the peppers and tomatoes with salt and pepper, then stir the olive oil through thoroughly before piling the mixture onto a serving plate. Arrange the anchovies and cheese over the top, then scatter with the chopped oregano. Set the salad aside for 30 minutes before serving to let the flavors develop.

MARINATED PEPPERS

This recipe is one that my family often makes at the end of summer when there is a glut of peppers. This salad is great with fried eggs and potatoes for lunch, or on its own as an appetizer.

Serves 4
6 red bell peppers (or a mix of whatever
   peppers you have)
6 tablespoons extra virgin olive oil
1 tablespoon sherry vinegar
1 garlic clove, finely chopped
½ small white onion, chopped
salt and freshly ground black pepper
1 flat-leaf parsley sprig

Coat the peppers with 1 or 2 tablespoons of olive oil and place them under a preheated broiler to blister the skin. Turn them once or twice—you don't want the flesh to turn to charcoal.

Once the peppers are black and blistered, you can either place them in a deep bowl and cover with plastic wrap or tie them up in a plastic bag. Either method ensures that as the peppers cool, the moisture condenses—and helps separate the skin from the flesh.

Once cool enough to handle, peel the skins off the peppers and remove the pith and seeds. At the same time, save the juices, straining them to remove any remaining debris. Next mix together the peppers, their juices, vinegar, garlic, the remainder of the oil, and the onion. Season to taste with salt and pepper and let marinate for about 6 hours in the fridge. When you are ready to serve, decorate with some parsley.

GRILLED MIXED VEGETABLE SALAD

Escalivada is a Catalan grilled salad, but actually there are lots of variations from all over Spain. It's ideal to make at a barbecue—the charcoal adds a lovely smokiness to the grilled vegetables. You could roast the vegetables in the oven, but the flavor won't be the same.

Purists never put vinegar in this salad, but I like to marinate the cooked vegetables to brighten and develop the flavors. In Catalonia they eat the warm salad immediately.

Serves 6

6 tablespoons extra virgin
  olive oil
3 eggplants
4 red bell peppers
3 red onions, unpeeled
1 head of garlic, plus
  3 cloves for the eggplants
3 ripe tomatoes
1 bunch of scallions
1 tablespoon sherry vinegar
salt and freshly ground
  black pepper

First of all, check the heat of the charcoal—if you can keep your hand over the coals for a count of six, then the temperature is right. You want a lower heat than when grilling meat.

Use 1 tablespoon of the oil to coat the eggplants, peppers, onions, and garlic head and place them whole on the grill. When I am doing this on the grill, I make a slit in each eggplant lengthwise and then peel 3 cloves of garlic and put one inside each eggplant before grilling them. (I got this tip from David Eyre; thanks David.) Once cooked, the eggplants have a wonderful subtle garlic flavor.

Turn the vegetables every 5 minutes or so, until they are properly cooked—you want them black on the outside and soft in the middle. This will take a good 30 minutes. Add the tomatoes and scallions about 10 minutes before you think the other vegetables will be ready.

Place all the vegetables into a large bowl, cover with plastic wrap, and let them sweat for about 10 minutes. Don't leave them until they're cold; they should be just hot enough to handle.

Take a bowl of water with which to wash your hands. Peel the onions and cut them up into wedges. Next, remove and discard the garlic from the eggplants, then peel off the skin—you can use your fingers, hence the bowl of water. Now do the tomatoes, leaving the peppers until last because they need longer sweating to remove the skins. Don't throw away the juices created from all this peeling— use it as part of the salad. Coarsely chop the eggplants, tomatoes, and peppers.

Now squeeze the garlic flesh out of the skins, and mash it to a purée in a small bowl. Whisk in the vinegar followed by the rest of the oil to make an emulsion. Season to taste with salt and pepper.

Stir the garlic dressing into the vegetables, and either eat immediately or let marinate for a couple of hours.

SUMMER VEGETABLE STEW

Pisto manchego is the Spanish equivalent of ratatouille. In fact, there are many versions of this combination of peppers, zucchini, and tomato all around the Mediterranean. It is an excellent dish when you have a glut of vegetables or when they may have grown a bit big. Either way, this is a great recipe to use them up. You don't have to be precise about quantities, and you can add eggplant if you want. The most important thing is the long, slow cooking, honoring the traditional Spanish ways of my mother and grandmother.

I love the richness of duck eggs, but if you don't have access to them, then of course free-range hen eggs are fine.

Serves 4

4 tablespoons extra virgin olive oil

2 garlic cloves, finely chopped

1 onion, diced

4 large flavorful tomatoes, chopped

1 bay leaf

2 green bell peppers, cubed

2 red bell peppers, cubed

salt and freshly ground black pepper

4 medium zucchini, cubed

olive oil, for frying

4 free-range duck or hen eggs

4 slices of good-quality bread

5 flat-leaf parsley sprigs, chopped

Heat the oil in a large frying pan, add the garlic and onion, and gently sauté until soft and pale, not golden. Now add the tomatoes and bay leaf and reduce to a sauce. Next, stir in the green and red peppers, season with salt and pepper, and cover and cook over low heat until soft. This will take about 10 minutes.

Once the peppers are cooked, add the zucchini, cover the pan with a lid, and cook very slowly for another 30 to 40 minutes, stirring occasionally. The end result should be sticky and luscious.

Cook the eggs as described on page 30, and toast the bread. Lay a slice of toast on each plate, ladle on the pisto, then slide a fried egg on top. Drizzle with a little olive oil and sprinkle chopped parsley over everything.

GRILLED POUSSIN WITH SALVITXADA SALSA

This is a great recipe to use for a barbecue. *Salvitxada* is a Catalan sauce, very similar to the more famous romesco sauce (see page 19), but with the addition of chile peppers and a little more olive oil and vinegar. Traditionally, *salvitxada* is served with grilled *calçots*, a Catalan spring vegetable that's a sort of cross between a scallion and a leek, but I like it with grilled chicken as well.

Serves 4
4 poussins

marinade
4 tablespoons extra virgin
   olive oil
4 marjoram sprigs, leaves
   stripped
juice and zest of 1 lemon
1 red chile, seeds removed
   and finely chopped
2 garlic cloves, finely chopped
freshly ground black pepper

salvitxada sauce
4 large ripe tomatoes
3 garlic cloves
1 red chile pepper
¼ cup toasted almonds
¼ cup toasted hazelnuts
2 dried ñora peppers,
   soaked for 2 hours in warm
   water, drained
1 slice of toast
4 tablespoons extra virgin
   olive oil
2 tablespoons sherry vinegar
sea salt

Ask your butcher to butterfly the poussins—the only bones you want left in the birds are the legs and wings. Mix the marinade ingredients together in a bowl and then rub it into the poussins. Cover and let marinate in the fridge for 12 hours.

Bring the poussins to room temperature and place on a medium to hot grill on the barbecue and brown the meat—this will take about 5 minutes on each side. Alternatively, the poussins can be roasted in the oven at 425°F for 7 minutes.

Meanwhile, grill the tomatoes until the skins are blackened and the flesh is cooked. Roast the garlic in their skins until they are soft inside. Grill the red chile until its skin is blistered.

For this sauce, you can use either a pestle and mortar (which results in a more authentic texture and is good for cooks in need of getting rid of a little stress) or, if you are in a hurry, a food processor. I'll assume it's the latter.

First, pulse the nuts to make a rough, chunky mixture. Then, remove the skins of the tomatoes and quarter them. Squeeze the garlic cloves out of their skins and scrape the flesh from the peppers. Add the tomatoes, garlic, and pepper flesh to the processor, along with the soaked ñora peppers, and pulse the mixture again. Tear up the toast and add this to the mixture. Process once more to reduce it to a coarse breadcrumb texture. Add the oil and vinegar and process just enough to mix it all together.

Season with salt to taste and serve with the poussins.

FISHING

I love to cook both sea and fresh water fish, but most of all, I love to cook fish that I have caught myself. Fishing is such a great mix of skill, contemplation, and the final adrenalin rush of actually catching supper.

Fish fresh from the sea remind me of summer vacations, while river fishing means time with my Dad. There's a big river in my region called the Tajo: it is slow flowing, meandering its way through mountainous gorges. My father and I used to go fishing in this river every Sunday morning before church for what the local folks call the *blah blah*, a big-mouthed fish introduced from America. For years I thought this was its real name, but blah blah is actually a corruption of its English name, the black bass trout.

Carp is also a common catch, with beautiful brown trout found further up river. In fact, Extremadura is a popular destination for fishing enthusiasts from all over Spain.

BAKED BROWN TROUT WITH BACON AND HERB SALAD

When I was about nine years old, I was sent to a summer camp for two weeks. Four other boys and I slept under the stars and spent our days swimming in mountain lakes and streams, where the trout would swim around our legs. I'd always feel a bit guilty because I knew one of them would end up on my plate. The camp was in the north of Extremadura in a place called Valle del Jerte, which is well known for its cherries. Luckily for us, our camp was surrounded by trees that produced cherries the size of small plums. So you can imagine supper: trout caught the hour before and a pile of fresh fruit picked straight off the tree. It was heaven.

Serves 4

4 whole trout (approx. 10oz each), cleaned
8 slices smoked bacon
sea salt
2 heads romaine lettuce, sliced
handful of mixed herbs, such as chervil, basil, and flat-leaf parsley

This is a quick dish to make. First preheat the oven to 400°F.

Place 2 slices of bacon lengthwise in the cavity of each trout and use a cocktail stick or toothpick to close the belly. Sprinkle salt sparingly on both sides of the fish and pat into the skin.

Oil a baking sheet, arrange the fish evenly across it, and bake for 12 to 15 minutes.

Mix the lettuce and herbs together, and dress with 4 tablespoons extra virgin olive oil and 2 tablespoons white vinegar, salt and pepper. Divide between four plates. Remove the cocktail sticks and place each fish next to the salad. Serve immediately.

SALMON CARPACCIO WITH ALMOND SALAD

Wild salmon is quite common in northern Spain, and it is at its best in early summer. Wild salmon is an expensive but wonderful-tasting fish, and this recipe is a great way of honoring it.

Make sure you buy line-caught rather than trawler-caught salmon. For this recipe you don't need the prime middle cut; the tail will do. Ask your fishmonger to fillet it for you.

Serves 4

salmon carpaccio
14oz salmon tail (2 fillets)
6 tablespoons extra virgin
   olive oil
6 tablespoons freshly
   squeezed orange juice

almond salad
½ cup flaked almonds
generous handful of frisée
   salad leaves
10 chive stalks, finely
   snipped
4 tablespoons extra virgin
   olive oil
2 tablespoons Moscatel
   white wine vinegar
salt and freshly ground
   black pepper

Get a really sharp knife and thinly slice the salmon toward the tail. The technique is to try and skim the flesh with the knife at around a 20° angle; don't chop downward. Your first couple of slices may be a bit ragged, but that won't affect the taste—you'll get better the more you practice. Place the slices of salmon on a serving plate immediately, arranging them around the edge to leave room for the salad in the middle.

Whisk together the olive oil and orange juice and pour this mixture over the salmon. Let the fish marinate in the dressing for 30 minutes.

Heat a heavy-bottomed frying pan and dry-fry the almonds until they are nicely golden. This will take 2 minutes over medium heat, but remember that the almonds will keep cooking in the pan, so remove them as soon as you think they're done. Let cool.

Mix the salad leaves, almonds, and chives together, then make the dressing by whisking together the oil and vinegar. Pour the dressing over the top of the salad mixture.

Pile the salad in the center of the salmon slices. Sprinkle everything with a pinch of salt and a couple of twists of freshly ground black pepper and serve.

FRESHWATER CRAYFISH WITH SPICY TOMATO SAUCE

Crayfish can be a menace in rivers across the world. They are aggressive and breed quickly—the only good thing about them is that they taste wonderful. So eat as many as you can get ahold of!

Back home, we use baskets with some bait such as an old piece of chicken soaked in vinegar to make it smelly. This is thrown into the river the night before and—*y listo*—the next morning the baskets are bursting with crayfish.

The basic tomato sauce described here can be used in lots of different ways—spread on crusty bread, stirred into stews, etc.—but here it is used as part of the *sofrito*, which is a quintessentially Spanish term to describe the preparation of fried onions, garlic, and other ingredients (often tomato) at the beginning of a dish.

Serves 4

basic tomato sauce: 1¼ cups
2 tablespoons extra virgin
    olive oil
1 small onion, chopped
2 garlic cloves, chopped
26oz ripe tomatoes, peeled
    and chopped
1 tablespoon superfine sugar
salt and freshly ground
    black pepper

sofrito
2 tablespoons extra virgin
    olive oil
1 onion, finely sliced
1 garlic clove, sliced
1 large carrot, finely diced
1 teaspoon spanish smoked
    paprika (hot)
6 tablespoons brandy

½ cup vegetable stock
24 freshwater crayfish

To make the tomato sauce, heat the oil in a frying pan, add the onion and garlic, and sauté until soft and golden. Stir in the chopped tomatoes, sugar, and half a teaspoon of salt, then let everything cook gently for about 40 minutes until most of the juices have evaporated. Adjust the seasoning.

To make the *sofrito*, heat the oil in a large frying pan and sauté the onion and garlic until soft. Add the carrot and cook for another 3 minutes.

Stir in the paprika and cook for 20 seconds before pouring in the brandy. Let the alcohol evaporate—this will take about 2 minutes—and then add the tomato sauce and the stock. Give everything a good stir, bring the mixture to a boil, and then add the crayfish. Cover and continue to cook for another 10 minutes. The crayfish will change from green to a lovely reddish-orange color.

These hooligans of the river bed need to be eaten on a hot sunny day, with lots of really good crusty bread and a pint of cold beer.

GRILLED TUNA STEAK WITH ROAST TOMATOES

Tuna is a fantastic, meaty fish that is much revered in Spain. Wherever you live, try to make sure that your tuna is the yellow fin variety, which is less endangered than the others.

Serves 4

24 cherry tomatoes

2 garlic cloves, finely chopped

6 tablespoons extra virgin olive oil

2 oregano or marjoram sprigs, leaves stripped

1 tablespoon capers

26 Kalamata black olives, pitted

4 tuna steaks (approx. 9oz each)

Preheat the oven to 300°F.

Mix the cherry tomatoes, garlic, 5 tablespoons of the oil, and oregano (or marjoram) in a bowl before pouring everything onto a baking sheet. Roast for about 15 to 20 minutes, until the tomatoes look as though they are about to collapse and their skins are crinkled. Remove from the oven and set aside to cool.

Once they've cooled, transfer the tomatoes to a salad bowl, scraping in the delicious juices from the baking sheet, then stir in the capers and olives.

Ideally, for the next stage you should use a ridged griddle pan. If you don't have one of these, use a heavy-duty cast-iron frying pan instead. Heat the griddle pan until it's very hot before adding the remaining oil. Season the tuna steaks and add them to the pan without overcrowding (but if you're using a large outdoor grill, then of course they can be cooked all at the same time). I love rare tuna, which means that the steaks need only a minute or so on each side, but grill the tuna according to how well cooked you like them.

Place the tuna steaks on plates and pile the tomatoes on top and around the sides of the steaks. Eat immediately.

MACKEREL ESCABECHE

I originally developed this recipe for carp; it's a sustainable fish that in my opinion should be eaten more by everyone. The flaky, slightly fatty flesh is similar to that of wild sea bream, and this method of pickling the fish really suits its texture. Since carp can be difficult to find in parts of the US, here we use the abundant and very delicious mackerel.

Serves 4

2 whole mackerel (approx. 5oz each), cleaned and filleted
salt and freshly ground black pepper
½ cup flour
10 tablespoons extra virgin olive oil
1 small Spanish onion, finely sliced
2 garlic cloves, sliced
1 large carrot, cut into batons
1 celery rib, cut into batons
handful of mixed herbs, such as bay leaf, thyme, and rosemary
1 teaspoon black peppercorns
3 tablespoons white wine vinegar
3 tablespoons dry white wine
⅔ cup water

Season the mackerel fillets, patting the salt and pepper firmly into the flesh. Then dunk the fillets into the flour, making sure both sides are lightly covered.

Heat 2 tablespoons of oil in a sauté pan. When it starts to shimmer, add the fillets and brown for about 2 minutes on each side. Set aside in a shallow gratin dish and cover with foil while you make the escabeche.

In a clean frying pan, add 2 more tablespoons of oil, then cook all the vegetables until soft and golden. This will take about 5 to 6 minutes. Stir in the herbs and peppercorns, then pour in the remainder of the oil, vinegar, and white wine. Let everything bubble until the alcohol has evaporated—this will take about 2 minutes. Add the water and simmer for another 3 minutes. Adjust the seasoning and pour this mixture over the mackerel fillets.

You can eat this immediately, or cold: it's delicious either way.

GRILLED MACKEREL WITH CRISPY SERRANO HAM AND WATERCRESS SALAD

This recipe is easy and elegant. It is something of a mystery to me why mackerel is not a widely popular dish; it is excellent value and, most importantly, tastes wonderful.

Serves 4

6 tablespoons extra virgin olive oil

8 slices of Serrano ham

4 small mackerel, filleted

salt and freshly ground black pepper

watercress salad

3 tablespoons extra virgin olive oil

1 tablespoon Moscatel white wine vinegar

salt and freshly ground black pepper

bunch of watercress, washed

$\frac{2}{3}$ cup flaked almonds, toasted

Preheat the broiler.

Heat the olive oil in a small frying pan over medium-high heat. Cook the ham until it's crispy. Set the slices aside on paper towels to drain off any excess oil while you cook the mackerel.

Season the fillets with salt and pepper, then brush a tiny amount of oil onto the skin of the fillets; the flesh is quite oily already. Place the mackerel, skin-side down, on a baking sheet and then slide under the broiler. Cook for 2 minutes, turn the fillets over, and cook for another 3 minutes.

For the salad, simply make the vinaigrette by whisking together the oil, vinegar, and salt and pepper, then pour it over the watercress and almonds in a bowl. Toss well.

Divide the salad between four plates. Arrange two mackerel fillets on each plate, alongside the salad, then gently rest a ham slice on top and serve.

RED MULLET WITH SLICED POTATOES AND BLACK OLIVES

The first time I had red mullet was in El Puerto de Santa María, a town close to Cádiz where the inhabitants seem to drink Fino sherry and eat gorgeous fish all day, every day of the year.

The best kind of red mullet comes from the Mediterranean, and there are in fact two varieties: *Mullus surmuletus*, which likes to hang out near rocks, living off smaller fish and crustaceans; and *Mullus barbatus*, which lives in sandy waters eating all kinds of things.

Fishmongers tend not to distinguish between the two, selling simply "red mullet," but it is well worth asking for the rock-loving version as it has a much sweeter, clearer flavor. You can identify the fish by the stripes on the first dorsal fin and, when fresh, three or four yellow streaks along its sides. Its profile is slightly more elongated and less snub-nosed than its cousin.

Red mullet has such a beautiful sweet flavor that it doesn't need anything complicated done to it, just a simple pan-fry. I think this combination of potatoes and olives showcases the fish to perfection.

The fish should have been caught on the day you buy them, and buy the biggest specimens you can find. Each fish should weigh around 14oz prior to filleting. Get your fishmonger to fillet them for you—each fish will give you two fillets of around 3½oz each.

Serves 4

3 medium potatoes, peeled
5 tablespoons extra virgin olive oil
2 garlic cloves, chopped
1 thyme sprig, leaves only
salt and freshly ground black pepper
30 Kalamata black olives, pitted
20 chive stalks, chopped
4 x 14oz red mullet, filleted
olive oil, for frying

Preheat the oven to 400°F.

Slice the potatoes as thinly as possible (use a mandolin if you have one), then mix with 2 tablespoons of olive oil, the chopped garlic, and thyme leaves. Season with salt and pepper, then spread the mixture over a greased baking sheet. Bake for about 15 minutes, until the potatoes are cooked.

Meanwhile, process the olives and half the chives with the remaining olive oil in a food processor to make a thick purée.

Season the fillets with salt and pepper. Heat the remaining 2 tablespoons of olive oil in a frying pan until medium—the oil should be shimmering but not smoking—and fry the mullet for 2 minutes skin-side down, then turn over and fry for another minute. You want a crispy skin.

Divide the potatoes between four plates, place two fillets on top of each mound, and, using a teaspoon, drizzle the plate with the olive purée. Scatter the remaining chives over everything and eat immediately.

PAN-FRIED SEA BASS WITH FENNEL AND BLACK OLIVE SALAD

Wild fennel is delicious in salads, but bulb fennel is not a common vegetable in Spain—I first came across it in London, and it is widely available in the US.

Serves 4

fennel and olive salad

2 plump fennel bulbs
1 lemon
20 Kalamata black
   olives, pitted
3 tablespoons extra virgin
   olive oil, plus extra for
   serving
salt and freshly ground
   black pepper

sea bass

3 tablespoons extra virgin
   olive oil
4 fillets of sea bass
   (approx. 5oz each)
5 flat-leaf parsley sprigs,
   chopped

First, make the fennel salad. Remove any discolored outer leaves from the fennel, then slice the bulbs as thinly as possible, using either a very sharp knife or a mandolin. Place the slices into water, add a good squeeze of lemon juice, and leave it for an hour: this makes the fennel nice and crunchy.

When you are ready to assemble the salad, drain the fennel slices and pat them dry with a clean kitchen towel. Then simply mix the fennel, olives, oil, and a pinch of salt in a large bowl, along with another squeeze of lemon juice. Season with black pepper and set aside while you pan-fry the sea bass.

Heat the olive oil in a large frying pan until it shimmers. Season the sea bass fillets sparingly with salt and then slide them skin-side down into the oil. Cook for 3 minutes, turn the fillets over, and cook for another minute.

Distribute the salad between four plates, and place the fillet on top. Drizzle a tiny bit of olive oil over the fish and scatter parsley over the top. Eat immediately.

BUTTERFLIED SARDINES WITH SALSA VERDE AND TOMATO SALAD

I love sardines. Whenever my mother used to come back from the market with a basket of fish, she'd pick out a sardine, clean it and strip its backbone out, and then I'd eat it raw. I love eating them whole, too: just chuck some sardines, guts still in, onto the grill and cook until the skins are really crisp; the intestines give an earthy bitterness to the flesh. For this recipe, ask your fishmonger to clean and butterfly the fish for you. My village, Talaván, has a sardine fiesta at the beginning of Lent. There's a communal barbecue in the main square, where masses of local red wine accompanies great chunks of bread with the grilled sardines squished between the slices. Everyone's house smells of fried fish for a week afterward!

Serves 4

salsa verde

4 sprigs each of parsley, mint, and basil
approx. 4 tablespoons extra virgin olive oil
½ red chile, seeds removed
1in piece of lemon peel
4 anchovy fillets in olive oil
1 tablespoon salted capers, rinsed
juice of ½ lemon

tomato salad

8oz cherry plum tomatoes
1 small red onion, finely sliced
4 tablespoons extra virgin olive oil
2 tablespoons Cabernet red wine vinegar

sardines

olive oil, for frying
8 medium sardines
salt and ground black pepper
⅔ cup flour
3 large eggs, beaten
2 marjoram sprigs, leaves stripped and chopped

First, make the salsa verde. Bring some water to a boil in a small saucepan and blanch the herbs for 30 seconds. Remove the herbs and immediately plunge them into a bowl of iced water. Leave for a minute or two. This ensures that the salsa stays a lovely green color.

Having drained the herbs, add them to a food processor along with the oil, chile, lemon peel, and the anchovies. Process everything to a paste. Scrape the sauce into a bowl before stirring in the capers and the lemon juice. This salsa will keep for 4 days in the fridge—and it's also good with roast chicken.

Next, prepare the tomato salad: slice the tomatoes (in half will do) and place in a bowl with the sliced onion. Whisk together the oil and vinegar to make a vinaigrette and mix it through the salad. Season with salt and pepper.

Heat some oil in a frying pan over medium heat—you want it to be shimmering with heat so that if you drop in a tiny bit of beaten egg, it sizzles vigorously.

Season the fish fillets with salt and pepper, then dip them in the flour, followed by the egg. Cook one fillet at a time. The thing to remember about frying fish is that it cooks very quickly, so it's difficult to be exact about how long you should cook each fillet for—you are aiming for a nice golden color. As a rough guide, for fish of this size, estimate 1 to 2 minutes cooking time. Once cooked, transfer the fillets onto paper towels to absorb the excess oil.

Place two sardines on each plate, drizzle over some salsa verde, and arrange a couple of spoonfuls of tomato salad on one side. Sprinkle marjoram over everything and eat immediately.

MARINATED ANCHOVIES

This is more of a story than a recipe, because it's a dish for when you have managed to buy the anchovies directly from the boat. It is one of my favorite tapas dishes. But while marinated anchovies are most often served as tapas accompanied by green olives, they also make a great salad with piquillo peppers, toasted walnuts, and fresh herbs (see page 127).

The anchovies have to be absolutely fresh, because they aren't cooked as such—they're cured in the vinegar. What is more, it's impossible to be exact with the quantities; it's more important to use your judgement. You'll need about 12oz anchovies for four people, and sufficient quantities of oil and vinegar to keep the fillets covered in marinade—and this depends on the size and shape of the bowls you're using.

The first task is to fillet all the anchovies and then submerge them in a bowl of white wine vinegar to which you have added a teaspoon of salt. Make sure the fillets are fully submerged in the vinegar, cover, and then let marinate in the fridge for a minimum of 6 hours— overnight is best.

After a good long pickle, rinse the fish in lots of cold water and pat dry with a kitchen towel. The fillets now go into another marinade of olive oil, a handful of chopped flat-leaf parsley, and 2 chopped garlic cloves. There are two important things to remember: firstly, to use a glass or plastic container, not a metal one; secondly, arrange the anchovy fillets like soldiers, skin-side down—if necessary, make a double layer of the fish. Sprinkle the garlic and parsley evenly over the fish before pouring over sufficient olive oil to submerge them completely. Cover the container and leave it for one day. They will keep for at least 3 or 4 days in the fridge. Eat the fish using a cocktail stick—or your fingers— but not a fork, please!

FISH STEW

Caldereta de pescado, or fish stew, reminds me of holidays—going to a really good fish market, picking out the best from the day's catch, then taking it all back home to play with.

This stew doesn't need complicated equipment or lots of time, so it's ideal to serve when friends come over for supper. Even better, it's easy to prepare and a complete meal in itself. It's based on a Catalan recipe that I came across on one of those aforementioned holidays.

Picada is a Catalan term for a mixture of nuts, breadcrumbs, and spices used to thicken stews.

Serves 4

picada
4 tablespoons extra virgin
  olive oil
¼ cup almonds
½ slice of white bread, 2 or
  3 days old, torn up
2 garlic cloves

fish stew
1 small onion, chopped
2 very ripe large tomatoes,
  chopped
1 red chile, seeds removed
  and diced
1 bay leaf
1 quart fish stock
2 medium potatoes, peeled
  and sliced ½in thick
20 saffron threads
14oz mixture of firm-fleshed
  fish, such as hake and
  sea bream
8 raw shrimp (shells on)
10oz clams (shells on)
handful of chopped flat-leaf
  parsley or cilantro
extra virgin olive oil,
  for drizzling

First make the *picada*. Heat the olive oil in a large saucepan, then add the almonds, bread, and garlic and cook until everything is golden—this will take 4 to 5 minutes.

Remove the ingredients from the pan, trying to leave as much oil behind as possible, and then either pound the mixture using a pestle and mortar to make a chunky paste, or process it in a food processor.

Now for the stew. Add the onions to the same pan and sauté for about 5 minutes, until soft, before stirring in the chopped tomatoes. Let the juices evaporate a little, then add the chile, bay leaf, and stock. Bring to a boil and add the potato slices and saffron, then let the mixture simmer gently for about 10 minutes, until the potatoes are soft. Add the picada and stir well to ensure that it is well mixed into the cooking juices.

Five minutes before serving, add the fish and shellfish. Don't add everything all at once: start with the fish steaks, largest first, then 1 minute later the shrimp, followed by the clams; the latter will take only about a minute to open (discard any that don't).

Serve immediately with a sprinkling of chopped parsley—or fresh cilantro, which is a Portuguese twist—and a drizzle of extra virgin olive oil.

CRISPY SHRIMP FRITTERS

I love these fritters, known as *tortillas de camarones* in Spain. One of the ways I like to relax when I'm on vacation in El Puerto de Santa María is to watch the world go by with an ice-cold beer in one hand and a plate of these delicious hot fritters within easy reach of the other. My favorite bar is the trendy La Rufana, which makes the best fritters.

The fish markets in and around Cádiz all sell glass shrimp, or *camarones*, often still alive, leaping around in the large plastic bowls where they have been casually tossed. Outside Spain, though, I recommend you buy the freshest shrimp you can find at your local supermarket.

Serves 4 to 6
(makes 12 fritters)

batter
1 cup flour
½ teaspoon baking soda
¼ teaspoon fine salt
⅔ cup water
olive oil, for frying

shrimp mixture
1 shallot (or ½ red onion),
  diced as small as possible
1 tablespoon extra virgin
  olive oil
7oz shrimp, peeled
  and cooked
½ teaspoon cayenne pepper
handful of flat-leaf parsley,
  finely chopped

Sift the flour, baking soda, and salt into a bowl. Slowly add the water, stirring with a wooden spoon as you do so. The batter should be easy to pour, similar to heavy cream in consistency. Add a little more water if necessary. If you have the time, let the batter sit for 30 minutes or so in the fridge.

Sauté the shallot or onion in the olive oil for about 5 minutes, until soft and pale. Then mix with the shrimp, cayenne, and parsley in a bowl.

When you are ready to cook, give the batter a good stir and fold in the shrimp mixture.

Heat some olive oil, about ½in deep, in a small, non-stick frying pan. When the oil starts to shimmer, ladle a spoonful of the mixture into the oil and spread it out gently to form a small, flat pancake roughly 2in in diameter. Don't feel tempted to make big fritters, as they are tricky to turn over.

When the fritter has formed a nice golden brown crust on the underside—which will take about 90 seconds—turn it over and brown the other side. Drain on paper towels.

Repeat with the rest of the mixture, but don't try to make too many at once; otherwise the oil temperature will drop and you will end up with greasy fritters. It is better to have guests standing at the ready with their plates, waiting for you to dish them out.

TAPAS: MY FAVORITE PASTIME

"Tapas, a favorite pastime?" I hear you ask. "Isn't tapas a way of presenting food?" To be sure, but for the Spanish, tapas is how we socialize with our friends. Let me tell you about a visit home last summer.

My great friends Burgos and Anabel came over for the evening. It was a last-minute arrangement and they did not arrive until ten thirty, perhaps a bit late even by Spanish standards, with their very alert five-year-old son in tow. We wandered off to one of the six bars in the village, where we settled down outside to drink Coke or beers, and nibbled on freshly made chips, olives, and boiled white beans called *altramuces*. Meanwhile, the children ran about kicking a soccer ball.

Around midnight, our tummies were still rumbling, so we headed back to our small internal courtyard. I hadn't planned or prepared any food, but my mother happened to have made ham croquettes earlier that day (for my fast-growing nephew Juan, who eats them by the dozen); and from the pantry we produced some tortillas, slices of cured pork called *lomo Ibérico*, tomatoes, and garlic from the vegetable garden—hastily made into a salad—and a can of clams. We opened a couple of bottles of good red wine, crammed round the table,

and chatted away for another couple of hours. We finished the evening with a large bowl of locally grown, deliciously sweet cherries, and a gooey, pungent Torta del Casar sheep cheese picked up from the cheesemaker's that morning.

The village square was still full of people when my friends waved their goodbyes in the early hours.

I love relaxed and spontaneous occasions like this, and the key is: the food has to be good, but it's your friends who matter. This is a small-village version of tapas. If I lived somewhere like Seville, we would have visited a few more bars that specialize in different types of tapas—one for ham, another for croquettes, and so on.

So, if you want to do tapas at home, it has to be easy—please don't spend two days preparing loads of different dishes. Buy the best-quality Ibérico ham and charcuterie; cheeses—cut to order, not pre-sliced and wrapped in plastic; and then choose a couple of dishes that can be made in advance. The chicory and blue cheese salad on page 28 is just one example of a great tapas recipe from this book. And get your friends to bring something—if they are like mine, they'll be happy to. Above all, enjoy yourself.

Disfruta!

CHERRY SANGRIA

I love sangria. The trouble is that when you make sangria for a party, the temptation is to use cheap ingredients, and this always means that your hangover will be worse. I have had years of experience of this, as it's the beverage of choice in my village whenever there's a fiesta and, of course, everyone drinks too much in the excitement and the sunshine. But that is what sangria is all about!

There is no exact recipe. People often use fizzy lemonade as the mixer to dilute the potent wine and brandy potion. But if you think this is too sweet, you could use soda water. You can play with the quantities, but please warn your guests if you have put a large amount of spirits into the brew—it slides down so nicely that they'll be drunk before they notice.

Serves 6

30 cherries, pitted
4 peaches, cut in segments
2 unwaxed oranges, juiced
  and peel removed
3 star anise
4 whole cloves
1 x 4in cinnamon stick
3 tablespoons brown sugar
1 bottle of good-quality
  Spanish wine
½ cup Brandy de Jerez
½ cup Cointreau
1¾ cups soda water,
  or to taste

Ideally, you should start making your sangria a day before you want to drink it. Begin by mixing together the cherries, peaches, orange juice and peel, spices, and sugar. Cover and let marinate in the fridge for 12 hours.

The next day, stir in the wine, brandy, Cointreau, and soda. Pour the sangria into a jug along with some ice, and give it a good stir. Make sure everyone gets some of the macerated fruit in their glass.

CHERRY MOUSSE

This is very easy to make. If you are in a hurry, you can omit the caramelized cherry step, but they make a nice surprise at the bottom of each glass.

Serves 6

caramelized cherries
½ cup superfine sugar
3 tablespoons water
juice of ½ lemon
24 cherries, pitted

cherry mousse
14oz cherries
zest of 1 lemon
½ cup superfine sugar
2 cups heavy whipping cream

¼ cup almonds, toasted

To make the caramelized cherries, heat a small saucepan over medium heat and dissolve the sugar in the water with a few drops of lemon juice. Continue to cook until the sugar turns a golden brown. Stir in the cherries and add the rest of the lemon juice. Cook for another minute. Remove from the heat, set aside to cool, and then divide the cherries between six wine glasses.

For the mousse, pit the cherries, then process them with a hand blender; this should give you about 9oz purée. Stir in the lemon zest and half of the sugar.

In another bowl, whip the cream with the remaining sugar until the cream has a light mousse-like texture. Lightly fold the cherry purée into the whipped cream and divide the mixture between the glasses.

Chill the mousse for a couple of hours. Just before serving, sprinkle the toasted almonds on top.

CREMA CATALANA AND CARAMELIZED FIGS

Traditionally, *crema catalana* was made only on St. Joseph's Day (the Spanish equivalent of Father's Day), on March 19th, by grandmothers and maiden aunts. These days, there are lots of powdered, just-add-milk custard preparations on the market—and my mother makes about a quart a day for my niece Marina and nephew Juan when they come to stay. They love it. Me, I prefer the traditional version.

While Spanish *crema catalana* and the French crème brûlée are different in some respects, the two desserts are very similar. Although, of course, *crema catalana* is more delicious! It is made from a mixture of milk and egg and is set by chilling, while crème brûlée is made with heavy cream and is set by baking in the oven, often in a bain-marie. The effect on people is the same: this dessert is always on the menu because it is hugely popular. I vary this recipe by serving it with caramelized figs.

Serves 4

custard
1 quart whole milk
peel of ½ lemon, pith removed
peel of ½ orange, pith removed
2in cinnamon stick
6 large free-range egg yolks
½ cup superfine sugar
½ cup cornstarch

caramelized figs
4 black figs
4 tablespoons soft brown sugar

Combine the milk, lemon and orange peels, and cinnamon in a heavy-bottomed saucepan. Place over medium heat and bring just to a boil, then remove and leave to infuse for an hour. Once cool, strain the milk through a fine sieve, discarding the solids.

Beat the egg yolks and superfine sugar until thick and pale, followed by the cornstarch, and then whisk in the infused milk. Return the custard to a clean heavy-based saucepan and cook, stirring continuously, for about 10 minutes over medium heat, until the mixture is thick and coats the back of a wooden spoon.

Cool slightly, then strain into a separate container. Pour the custard into four shallow ramekins and refrigerate until set; this should take 2 to 3 hours.

Slice the figs in quarters almost all the way through and place one on top of each *crema catalana*. Scatter the soft brown sugar over both the figs' gooey center and the custard. To caramelize the sugar, the easiest option is to use a blowtorch and blast the sugar until bubbling and golden; if you do not have one, place the custards under a preheated broiler and keep an eye on them to make sure they do not burn. Eat immediately.

SUMMER FRUIT SALAD WITH MINT AND OLIVE OIL

Forget whipped cream with your fruit salad, try olive oil—it's much more refreshing. This recipe is a favorite of my staff after a hot summer shift. Andalucía's Costa Tropical produces a wide range of fruits, and things like kiwi fruit and pineapple are no longer as exotic as they once were. Fruit in season is always the best, though, so adapt this salad to what is available and at its sweetest.

Serves 4

½ sweet pineapple, peeled
  and diced
2 peaches, pitted and sliced
2 kiwi fruit, peeled and sliced
16 strawberries, hulled and
  cut in half
handful of blueberries
4 tablespoons extra virgin
  olive oil
freshly ground black pepper
juice of 1 lime
3 mint sprigs, leaves
  stripped and chopped

Mix together everything except the mint, and let chill in the fridge for a few hours. Then, just before serving, stir in the chopped mint.

AUTUMN

**Mushrooms ✳ Chestnuts ✳ Pumpkins ✳ Garlic and Onion ✳
Piquillo Peppers ✳ Seafood and Fish ✳ Beef ✳
Smoked Paprika ✳ Rice ✳ Saffron ✳ Pears and Apples**

In America, the colors of autumn are browns, golds, and reds. We get those colors in Spain, too, but whereas the US fades beneath cloudy days, the sky in Spain returns to blue again after the heat-sapping white of summer. Appetites return, and recipes that I want to cook become more robust and warming.

Autumn is when the peppers used to make *pimentón de la Vera*, or smoked paprika, are harvested and smoked in Extremadura, while over in La Mancha farmers pick the crocus stamens, which give us the much-prized saffron. I cannot imagine cooking without these spices. There is the gentle sport of looking for mushrooms, although some years this doesn't happen if the weather has been too dry. The chestnuts, however, can always be relied upon, and they make a wonderful sweet, earthy addition to stews and soups.

Shellfish such as mussels and razor clams come back into season, so I am a happy man as the nights draw in.

MUSHROOM HUNTING

Advice on mushroom hunting usually starts or ends with "If you cannot identify a mushroom with certainty, do not eat it—you could die!" Alas, this ensures that, for most us, the only kind of mushroom hunting we do is the pick-your-own version in the supermarket aisles.

In my village in Extremadura, not everyone likes collecting mushrooms, but enthusiasts have their own secret locations, and even if you're their best friend they don't tell you about them. Mushrooms always seem to pop up overnight, so my father's preferred strategy is to say he's moving the cows from one field to another, first thing in the morning. He is usually up so early that no one notices he has taken the long route through the *dehesa*, or wooded pastures.

There are several things to take on a mushroom hunt. First, pack a knife, as mushrooms should not be pulled or torn from the ground. Then you should bring a suitable container, but plastic and lids are no good: mushrooms must be allowed to breathe. I usually borrow my mother's old-fashioned wicker basket—that is, if my dad hasn't gotten to it first.

You also need a sharp pair of eyes. I find mushroom hunting very similar to collecting shells on a beach; it takes a while for my eyes to adjust to picking out creamy bulges in the grass, and then it becomes compulsive. Worse than that, if I am with someone, it can get very competitive—who can fill up a basket first and so on—but I never pick all the mushrooms, as fungus-collecting etiquette demands that you leave some behind to spread their spores.

In my area of Extremadura, common mushrooms include field mushrooms and fairy ring mushrooms; more difficult to track down are the earthy-flavored, blue-stalked *pieds bleus* (also known as wood blewits), fabulous chanterelles, and, of course the best of the lot, *cèpes* (or porcini, as they are also known).

Mushroom hunting may be a scattered, secretive pleasure where I come from, but over in Catalonia everyone is mushroom-crazy, and there are traffic jams as people head for the foothills of the Pyrenees to bag themselves a few fungi.

Here, popular mushrooms include the hedgehog fungus (*Hydnum repandum*), known as *gamuza* in Spanish, a treasure that is around from late summer to late autumn. It can have a slightly bitter taste when raw, so it needs to be cooked. The same is true of the saffron milk cap (*Lactarius deliciosus*), or *niscalo* in Spanish, which is probably the most highly prized of all Spanish fungi, but only found in parts of the US. It "bleeds" an orange-red liquid when cut.

If you want to discover why towns hold festivals and restaurants devote entire menus to mushrooms, you either need to take a trip to Spain in November, or visit someone like my friend Tony Booth, who runs The Wild Mushroom Company in London's Borough Market. Wild mushrooms aren't cultivated, they are picked from the countryside in places like Poland, Estonia, and, of course, Spain. The key is finding trusted suppliers, which Tony over the years has edited, so he always has a terrific selection.

Field mushrooms or some of the more exotic, wild mushrooms don't need fancy cooking, as the following recipes demonstrate.

FRIED MUSHROOMS ON TOAST

Tony Booth likes his mushrooms simple, and this is one of his favorite tapas plates; he orders it whenever he comes into my restaurant after a busy day in London's Borough Market.

Served with a fried egg, this also makes a beautiful supper dish, and is ready in minutes.

Serves 4

12oz assorted wild mushrooms, e.g., chanterelles, wood blewit, and porcini
1 garlic clove, sliced
1 thyme sprig, leaves stripped
salt and freshly ground black pepper
2 tablespoons extra virgin olive oil
1 shallot, finely diced
4 slices of sourdough bread
3½oz Manchego cheese, shaved
white truffle oil

Clean the mushrooms with a damp cloth, trim off any woody stems, and then chop them all up into large pieces. In a large bowl, mix the mushrooms with the garlic, thyme, and some salt and pepper.

Heat the oil in a large frying pan or wok over medium heat and soften the shallot for 2 minutes. Turn the heat up to high, add the mushroom mixture, and cook for 3 minutes, stirring regularly, until cooked and just slightly caramelized.

Toast the bread, then lay the slices on four warmed plates. Divide the mushroom mixture between them. Shake a few drops of truffle oil over each serving, sprinkle the cheese on top, and eat immediately.

PORCINI WITH SHRIMP AND SERRANO HAM

Served with some crusty bread, this is a very easy supper dish, with a good balance of sweet, salty, and savory flavors.

Serves 4

2 tablespoons extra virgin olive oil
1 garlic clove, chopped
12oz fresh porcini mushrooms, sliced
salt and freshly ground black pepper
16 raw shrimp, peeled
4 tablespoons dry white wine
3oz Ibérico or Serrano ham, diced
5 flat-leaf parsley sprigs, chopped

In a wok or frying pan, heat the oil over medium heat and add the garlic. Cook for about 1 minute, and, before it turns golden, add the porcini and sauté briskly. Season with salt and pepper.

When the mushrooms start to turn brown, add the shrimp followed by the wine. Cook until the shrimp have turned pink and the wine has reduced a little—about 2 to 3 minutes.

Divide the mixture between four warmed plates. Scatter the diced ham and parsley over the top and serve immediately.

WILD MUSHROOMS WITH SCRAMBLED EGGS

For this recipe, try and get ahold of a mixture of fresh wild mushrooms, such as wood blewits, chanterelles, and porcini.

Serves 4

3 tablespoons extra virgin olive oil

2 garlic cloves, chopped

11oz wild mushrooms

salt and freshly ground black pepper

1 thyme sprig, leaves stripped

8 large free-range eggs

4 slices of good-quality bread

3½oz Manchego or similar aged sheep cheese, shaved

handful of chopped flat-leaf parsley

In a wok or frying pan, heat the olive oil over medium heat and add the garlic. Before it turns golden, add the mushrooms. Cook the mushrooms at a higher heat than you would if you just wanted them to sweat. Season with salt and pepper.

When the mushrooms start to turn a golden brown, add the thyme and reduce the heat. Break the eggs over the mushrooms, and stir continuously and smoothly until the eggs are cooked.

Toast the bread and lay on four plates. Spoon some scrambled egg onto each, top with the shaved cheese, and sprinkle with parsley. Eat immediately.

WILD MUSHROOM FIDEOS

Fideos are Spanish noodles, eaten all over Spain. These short pieces of slightly curved, thin pasta aren't available in US supermarkets, but that shouldn't stop you from trying out this excellent recipe—use spaghetti broken into short pieces instead; as long as you don't try and do large fistfuls of pasta all at once, it's easy to do.

The key difference between Italian pasta and Spanish fideos isn't the shape; it has to do with how they're used. We are all familiar with boiling our pasta in salted water and then mixing through a sauce of some kind. Fideos, however, are cooked in a stock along with the other ingredients. Italian minestrone soup is the exception that proves the rule! Vegetarians could use a mushroom stock and omit the chorizo.

Serves 4 to 6

fideos

3 tablespoons extra virgin olive oil
1 medium onion, finely chopped
3 garlic cloves, chopped
1 carrot, diced
2 spicy chorizo sausages, about 6oz each, chopped
2 thyme sprigs
1½lb mixture of wild mushrooms (such as chanterelles and morels), torn into chunks
1½ quarts chicken stock
14oz fideos, or similar short pasta

picada

½ cup toasted almond slivers
zest and juice of 1 lemon
small handful of flat-leaf parsley and mint, chopped
1 garlic clove
1 tablespoon extra virgin olive oil

Heat the oil in a sauté pan and cook the onion, garlic, and carrot over medium heat until soft and golden. Add the chorizo and cook for about 2 minutes before adding the thyme. Keep stirring while you add the wild mushrooms and continue to sauté for 4 minutes, or until they have collapsed a little. Pour in the stock and scrape up any bits sticking to the base of the pan. Bring everything to a simmer, spoon off any foam that has risen to the surface, and stir in the pasta. Cover and cook until the pasta is soft—not *al dente* in the Italian fashion—which will take about 12 to 15 minutes depending on the type of pasta you have used.

Use a hand blender or food processor to process the picada ingredients to a chunky salsa consistency. Remove the pasta from the heat and stir in the picada. Set aside for 5 minutes to let the mixture cool just a little and the flavors develop.

Divide the fideos between four warmed bowls, making sure you scoop up the mushrooms, which will have settled to the bottom of the pan.

CHESTNUTS

The European chestnut tree is also known as the Spanish chestnut, perhaps due to the large forests to be found in Galicia and, to a lesser extent, in Andalucía. You might suppose from its name that a chestnut is a nut. Well, its shape might suggest as much, but true nuts have a fat content of 45 to 55 percent and are low in carbohydrates, whereas the chestnut contains more like 1 percent fat and about 80 percent carbohydrate. It is about as starchy as wheat, so it's no surprise it's sometimes known as "the grain that grows on a tree."

I love raw chestnuts even though they are a bit difficult to peel, because they taste deliciously sweet. Of course, chestnuts are also very nice roasted: when it's frosty, what better way is there to keep your hands warm while keeping your tummy from rumbling? Chestnut vendors are a common sight on city street corners in Spain, and traditionally these toasty nibbles were given to churchgoers holding vigils on All Saints' Day.

The best thing about All Saints' Day for me as a child was the *carboteo*, or campfire picnic. Every year, family and friends went off into the countryside to gather chestnuts and firewood, and then we'd have a feast. It was the only occasion in the year when we kids were allowed to play with fire—or rather roast our chestnuts—and of course we loved it.

You can use chestnuts in a very similar way to potatoes; for example, they are excellent mashed and served with a game casserole. In the following recipe, they add a subtle, smoky sweetness to the mushroom soup.

MUSHROOM AND CHESTNUT SOUP

This is a really autumnal recipe. Try to use best-quality smoked bacon or pancetta if you can.

Serves 4

3 tablespoons extra virgin
  olive oil
2 garlic cloves, finely diced
14oz mixed mushrooms,
  chopped
7oz cooked and peeled
  chestnuts, coarsely
  crumbled
1 quart chicken stock, warmed
salt and freshly ground
  black pepper
4 slices smoked bacon or
  pancetta, chopped
½ teaspoon sherry vinegar
2 thyme sprigs, leaves stripped

Heat 2 tablespoons of the oil in a saucepan over medium heat and cook the garlic until soft. Stir in the mushrooms and cook until browned. Stir in the chestnuts and cook for another 3 minutes. Pour in the stock, season with salt and pepper, and simmer for 20 minutes.

Meanwhile, heat the remaining tablespoon of olive oil in a frying pan over medium to high heat and cook the bacon pieces until brown and crisp. Set aside to drain on paper towels.

Once the mushrooms are cooked, use a hand blender to purée the soup; add the vinegar, give it a stir, and adjust the seasoning if necessary. Divide the soup between four warmed bowls. Scatter the thyme leaves and bacon pieces over the top and eat immediately.

SQUASH AND PUMPKINS

In Spain we don't distinguish between winter squash and pumpkins, we use the generic term *calabazas*. I prefer this name because in English-speaking countries, the differences seem to be more a matter of plant-breeder branding than botany. Winter squash and pumpkins are gourds that belong to the same genus, and are relatives of cucumbers and melons.

Whatever you want to call them, *calabazas* originated in the Americas. It was Francisco Pizarro, the conquistador from Extremadura, who was responsible for introducing them to Spain from Peru. They weren't very popular at first, possibly because early varieties were prone to bitterness—and in fact, they were more valued for their seeds.

Calabazas are an early example of a super-veggie—or rather super-fruit, as technically, squashes are indeed fruit. Native American Indians called them "the apples of god" and believed that they increased fertility. They are certainly an excellent source of beta-carotene, and are also low in carbohydrates; in fact, their list of virtues is a long one. The only problem with them is that they are often difficult to peel.

You have several choices when it comes to removing the peel. You can, for example, remove the skins after cooking them, or instead learn to love eating the skin, as it is edible once cooked; or you can blanch the whole squash for 5 minutes in a covered saucepan, let cool, and then strip the skin with a potato peeler; or, simply take a large heavy knife and quarter the squash before carefully removing the skin with a sharp paring knife.

SQUASH AND FENNEL FRITTERS

You can use any dense-flesh variety of winter squash for this recipe, such as butternut or spaghetti. Also, there is no need to remove the peel.

Serves 6 as an appetizer
2 medium winter squash (approx. 1lb in total)
2 fennel bulbs
1 cup flour, seasoned with salt and pepper
2 large free-range eggs, beaten
olive oil, for frying

Halve the squash and scoop out the seeds. Cut the pieces in half again, and then slice across the segment to give ⅛in thick slices. Trim the base of the fennel bulbs, taking off only a minimal amount. Halve each bulb, then thinly slice each piece lengthwise: the leaves should remain attached to the base to create a kind of fan-shape slice.

Put the flour in one bowl, and the beaten eggs in another. Pour a generous quantity of olive oil into a frying pan (it should be about ⅛in deep), and heat over medium to high heat until the oil shimmers.

Dunk the vegetables slices first in the flour and then the beaten egg—and then slide several at a time into the oil. When the underside of a slice is golden, which will take 1 to 2 minutes, flip it over. Continue cooking for 1 more minute.

You will need to cook the squash and fennel in batches: drain the slices on paper towels after removing them from the oil, then place them in a warm oven while you cook the rest.

Serve immediately with *mojo de cilantro*.

MOJO DE CILANTRO

This salsa or dip is popular in the Canary Islands. If you substitute the fresh cilantro with parsley, it becomes *mojo verde*. Make it a couple of hours before you want to use it, to give the flavors a chance to develop. This recipe comes from my friend Miguel, who in turn got it from his grandmother. She insists that the only way to make this *mojo* is with a pestle and mortar. You can use less garlic if you prefer.

Serves 6
3 large garlic cloves, coarsely chopped
1 tablespoon coarse sea salt
large bunch of cilantro, leaves only
1 green chile, seeded and chopped
1 teaspoon ground cumin
½ cup extra virgin olive oil
1 tablespoon Moscatel or other white wine vinegar

Pound the garlic and salt together with a pestle and mortar. Once the garlic is reduced to a paste, add the cilantro and continue to crush the herb into the mixture until you have a mash. Add the chile and cumin and bash it into the mixture; then, slowly add the oil, pounding all the while, until you have a smooth sauce. The vinegar will eventually darken the vibrant green color of the *mojo*, so stir it in just before serving.

ROAST PUMPKIN SOUP WITH BLUE CHEESE

The pumpkins we get in Extremadura can grow into monsters, sometimes 90 pounds in weight. So, eating one is a village endeavor: whenever my mother harvests one, she distributes pieces to all her friends and neighbors. My dad grows two types—a long, marrow-shaped one that is better for roasting, and the round, Halloween variety that is best for soups, as in this recipe.

I like to use Picos Blue with this soup, but Stilton or Gorgonzola make good alternatives.

Serves 4

2lb pumpkin, peeled and cut into chunks

2 tablespoons extra virgin olive oil, plus extra for drizzling

2 garlic cloves, whole and unpeeled

1 rosemary sprig

salt and freshly ground black pepper

1 quart vegetable or chicken stock

4 slices of good-quality bread

4oz blue cheese, Picos Blue or similar

Preheat the oven to 425°F.

Take a large baking sheet or two and, using your hands, mix together the pumpkin chunks, olive oil, garlic, rosemary, and salt and pepper thoroughly. You want the pumpkin nicely coated with oil to ensure that it browns evenly. Spread out in a single layer on the sheet.

Place the vegetables into the oven and bake for 25 minutes, until the pumpkin has started to caramelize around the edges.

Once cooked, remove the garlic and the rosemary before decanting the vegetables into a large pan. Add the stock, then bring to a gentle boil and let it simmer for 5 minutes to blend the flavors. Purée the soup using a hand blender and adjust the seasoning.

Toast or fry the bread. Ladle out the soup into four warmed bowls. Crumble the cheese onto the toast, then gently float the slices on the soup, drizzle with a little olive oil and serve immediately.

CASTILLIAN GARLIC SOUP

Garlic soups are popular all over Spain. This is my favorite version. Its strong, warming flavors make it ideal for a cold autumn's night.

Serves 4
2 tablespoons olive oil
6 garlic cloves, sliced
3½oz Serrano ham, cubed
3½oz semi-cured chorizo, cubed
1 teaspoon spanish smoked paprika (mild)
1 quart chicken stock
2 slices country-style white bread
4 large free-range eggs

Heat the oil in a pan over medium heat and cook the garlic until it is soft and starts to golden. Now add the ham and chorizo and sauté the meat until brown around the edges—it will take about 3 minutes.

Remove the pan from the heat before adding the paprika (burnt paprika is the most horrible thing in the world) and give everything a good stir. Add the stock and return the pan to the heat. Boil for 4 or 5 minutes—remove any fat and foam with a spoon.

Tear the bread into chunks and add to the pan. The bread should be soggy but not dissolved when you serve the soup.

Carefully crack the eggs on to a saucer or ramekin and slide into the soup. Poach the eggs for 4 minutes. Serve immediately.

ONION SOUP

This soup was a favorite with the staff at the hotel where I worked in Extremadura; I first learnt how to make it in college, but I have since adapted the recipe. Aim for equal quantities of red and white onions.

Serves 4
4 tablespoons extra virgin olive oil
3 medium red onions, sliced
3 medium white onions, sliced
sea salt
6 tablespoons dry sherry, preferably
   Fino or Oloroso
1 quart chicken stock
4 slices of good-quality bread
1 garlic clove, halved
3oz fresh goat cheese
2 thyme sprigs, leaves stripped

Heat the oil over low heat then add the sliced onions. Season with salt and sauté for 25 minutes. Add the sherry and let the alcohol evaporate, which will take about 3 minutes. Add the stock and simmer for another 20 minutes—you want the onions to be very mushy.

Preheat the broiler. While it is heating, toast the bread and ladle the soup into four earthenware bowls.

Rub the four slices of toast with the garlic clove, spread with the goat cheese, then float each slice on top of the soup. Slide the bowls under the hot broiler—the soup is ready to serve when the cheese starts to turn a bit brown in places.

Scatter the thyme leaves over the toast and drizzle with a little olive oil, if you wish, and serve immediately.

MARINATED PIQUILLO PEPPERS

Piquillo peppers originate from Navarra and, as their name suggests, they are pointy red peppers. I love them because they are fleshy and juicy, which makes them ideal for roasting or grilling. If you cannot find the real thing, then Romano red peppers are an acceptable substitute.

This is a popular recipe all over Spain. You can serve the marinated peppers as an appetizer, or add them to salads, casseroles, or anything that suits your taste.

Serves 4

8 to 10 fresh piquillo peppers
6 tablespoons extra virgin
    olive oil
1 garlic clove, finely chopped
2 thyme sprigs, leaves
    stripped
5 flat-leaf parsley sprigs,
    finely chopped
salt and freshly ground
    black pepper

Preheat the broiler. Coat the peppers with 1 tablespoon of olive oil and slide them under the broiler to blister the skin. Make sure you turn them once or twice while they are cooking—you don't want the flesh to turn to charcoal.

When they are done, either put the peppers in a deep bowl and cover with plastic wrap or seal them in a plastic bag; both methods allow the peppers to cool and the moisture to condense. Once cool enough to handle, slide the skins off the peppers and remove the pith and seeds. Save any juices, straining them to remove any debris.

Now mix the peppers (and their juices), the remaining olive oil, garlic, and fresh herbs together. Season to taste with salt and pepper and let marinate for 6 hours in the fridge.

Stored in the fridge in an airtight container, the peppers should keep for at least three or four days.

ANCHOVY, PIQUILLO PEPPER, AND WALNUT SALAD

There's a roadside café on the main road from Madrid to Portugal, at junction 46, if you ever go that way. The place is littered with discarded paper napkins, old cigarette butts, and broken toothpicks. It's so busy that it feels like a train station, and you have to give the bar staff a determined stare if they're ever going to notice you. But keep trying, and make sure you ask for the *boquerones en vinagre*. They arrive (eventually), with a huge chunk of bread and no knife or fork. Don't worry, just use a toothpick and dive into the best marinated anchovies ever: plump and covered in juicy chunks of garlic and golden olive oil. The governor of Extremadura always stops here, which tells you how good they are.

The method for marinating anchovies is described on page 96, but these days the deli counters at some supermarkets have very acceptable anchovies, which are fine in this salad. If you can't find jars or cans of piquillo peppers, use jarred roasted red peppers instead.

Serves 4 as an appetizer

dressing
4 tablespoons extra virgin
  olive oil
2 tablespoons Cabernet
  red wine vinegar
1½oz toasted walnuts,
  broken into coarse pieces
freshly ground black pepper

3½oz red piquillo peppers
16 marinated anchovies
1 small red onion, finely
  sliced
handful of fresh herbs, such
  as mint, chervil, and flat-
  leaf parsley

First make the dressing: mix the oil, vinegar, and walnuts together, and season with a couple of twists of freshly ground black pepper.

Cut the piquillo peppers into ½in slices, then combine in a bowl with the anchovies, sliced onion, and herbs. Pour the dressing over the top, toss, and serve.

SMOKED PAPRIKA

Spanish smoked paprika, or *pimentón de la Vera*, is one of my favorite spices: just one whiff of its smoky sharpness and I feel hungry. *Pimentón* is the Spanish word for paprika, the vibrant, rust-red spice made by pulverizing dried peppers. But authentic *pimentón de la Vera* is particularly special: it is smoked, and is made solely in La Vera valley, about an hour's drive from my family's home.

Peppers (*pimientos*) grow easily all over Spain, but the peppers from Extremadura are special, thanks to how they were introduced to the country. Spanish conquistadores brought them back from Mexico in the 16th century. The peppers, along with potatoes and tomatoes, were a gift for the king and queen of Spain. Of course, the monarchs never got their own hands dirty, and instead gave the new-fangled vegetables to the monasteries, which became the custodians—and cultivators—of such discoveries.

One such monastery was in Yuste, in La Vera valley, where the monks didn't just cultivate the peppers, but also dried them and ground them into a powder, or *pimentón*. Eventually, the crop was adopted by local farmers, although it wasn't until the mid-19th century that the farmers began growing their peppers on a large scale and processing them into paprika. This spice is now La Vera's main source of income. (Curiously, tobacco, another New World introduction, is grown alongside the peppers and the two crops are harvested simultaneously).

Dotted beside the pepper-growing fields in La Vera are little smokehouses. These two-story buildings look normal on the outside, but inside the walls are totally black. In autumn, strings of fresh peppers are hung up in the rafters on the first floor, and then smoked over smoldering holm oak fires lit on the ground floor below. The peppers remain in the smokehouse for about two weeks As well as imbuing the fruit with a heavenly mellow flavor, this smoking process almost completely dehydrates the peppers and ensures that they stay fiery red rather than a dull brown color.

The peppers are then pulverized and ground to a soft powder. To check that the end result is the right consistency, the foreman presses a wooden stick, just like a rolling pin, into a mound of paprika to see if it is even and smooth. Most of the paprika is packed into large sacks destined for the sausage (*embutido*) and cured meats industry. Cooks buy the spice in pretty jars in varying sizes.

There are three versions of *pimentón de la Vera*—*dulce* (sweet and mild), *agridulce* (bittersweet and medium-hot), and *picante* (hot)—made from different varieties of pepper. It is up to you how to use them, but in Spain, the hot version tends to be used in winter soups and spicy chorizos. The sweet version has an extraordinary affinity with potatoes and firm-fleshed white meat such as octopus, rabbit, and chicken. The bittersweet paprika, meanwhile, finds its way into game and bean stews.

Unsmoked paprika is also made in Spain, but the only paprika I use in this book is smoked. You won't regret making it a permanent feature of your spice collection.

PAN-FRIED PAPRIKA CHICKEN WITH MASHED POTATOES

I prefer to use hot smoked paprika for this dish, but please use it with caution! Mashed potatoes made with olive oil is just gorgeous with this.

Serves 4

chicken

3 tablespoons extra virgin
   olive oil
4 garlic cloves, skins on
1 bay leaf
8 boneless chicken thighs,
   skin on and cut in half
salt and freshly ground
   black pepper
1 teaspoon spanish smoked
   paprika (hot)
6 tablespoons dry sherry,
   preferably Fino

mashed potatoes

4 large russet potatoes
4 garlic cloves, peeled
1 bay leaf
6 tablespoons extra virgin
   olive oil

First, you want to infuse the oil that the chicken is going to be cooked in with the flavors of the garlic and bay leaf. So, heat the oil over very low heat and add the garlic cloves and the bay leaf. It should take about 20 minutes to color the garlic, but do so only very slightly: it's a warm bath, not a frying pan experience. Once cooked, remove the garlic and bay leaf. Set the cloves to one side (you'll need them later).

Turn the heat up to high. Season the chicken with salt and pepper, add it the pan, and cook for 4 minutes before turning the pieces over—you want a nice crispy golden outside. Cook for another 4 minutes. Add the paprika and the sherry; give everything a good stir and let simmer gently for about 5 minutes.

For the mashed potatoes, peel the potatoes and cut them into large chunks. Boil with the garlic cloves, bay leaf, 2 tablespoons of the olive oil, and a pinch of salt. Once cooked, drain and remove the garlic and bay leaf. Mash the potatoes with the remaining olive oil, and keep going until you have made a smooth purée. Season with salt and pepper.

Spoon the mashed potatoes into the middle of a platter, place the chicken on top, and pour over the juices. Serve with the cooked garlic cloves.

GALICIAN-STYLE OCTOPUS

I love octopus. The first time I had this dish was on my first visit to Santiago de Compostela in Galicia, when I was a student. It was raining, the way it always seems to do in that part of Spain. I don't remember anything else, but the memory of that meal has stayed with me always.

The main obstacle to overcome with octopus is the preparation. Octopus can be tough, so there are several methods to tenderize it. The traditional way is to pound the (dead) octopus, which pulverizes the fibers. The other way, which I prefer, is to put the octopus in the freezer for two days. In other words, it's perfectly OK to buy your octopus already frozen! Just make sure that your supplier is a good one.

For this particular dish, you should use a mix of hot and mild smoked paprika to dust over the top of the octopus.

Serves 4

octopus
1 bay leaf
2 tablespoons black
   peppercorns
1 onion, coarsely chopped
1 leek, coarsely chopped
1 carrot, coarsely chopped
1 octopus (approx. 3lb)
10oz baby potatoes, cleaned
   but not peeled

dressing
½ teaspoon spanish smoked
   paprika (hot)
½ teaspoon spanish
   smoked paprika (mild)
4 tablespoons extra virgin
   olive oil
sea salt flakes
handful of chopped flat-
   leaf parsley

Put plenty of water in a large saucepan, add the bay leaf, peppercorns, onion, leek, and carrot, and bring to a boil. Take the octopus by the head and dunk the tentacles into the water 3 times. This keeps the tentacles from sticking as they cook. After the third dunk, make sure the octopus is wholly submerged and simmer gently for approximately 35 minutes, until it is tender. To be sure it is cooked, take a toothpick and push it into the flesh between the head and the tentacles. If you can push it in easily, it's done.

Scoop out the octopus with a couple of large wooden or steel spoons. The main thing to remember is to avoid touching the flesh until it's completely cold. If you do, the beautiful purple skin will peel away on your hands. Once it is cool, you can chop up the octopus into bite-size pieces.

Remove the vegetables and herbs from the octopus water and let the water cool. Once it's cold, add the potatoes. Boil until tender—about 15 minutes. Drain, and when they are cool enough to handle, cut them into thick slices.

Take a large platter—traditionally a wooden plate is used—and arrange the potatoes and chopped octopus on it. Dress with the paprika, followed by the oil, salt, and parsley.

Variation: you can also mix the octopus and potato together with some frisée lettuce to make a salad.

BASQUE TUNA AND POTATO STEW

This is another dish that uses both paprika and potato. Here, the sweetness is provided by tuna rather than octopus, and it's another match made in heaven. The stew is a typical fisherman's dish, a meal in itself. I like to make it for friends when they come over for a casual supper. It's easy, it's quick, and it's great with a bottle of Chacolí—a floral and dry white wine from the Basque Country. Mmmmm.

Serves 4

3 tablespoons extra virgin olive oil

2 onions, diced

3 tomatoes, grated or diced

2 green bell peppers, cut into strips

1 red bell pepper, cut into strips

2 teaspoons spanish smoked paprika (mild)

6 tablespoons dry white wine

4 medium floury potatoes, peeled

1 quart fish stock

sea salt

1¾lb fresh yellowfin tuna, cut into 1in cubes

Heat the oil in a large sauté pan, add the onion, and cook until golden brown—about 5 minutes. Add the tomatoes and peppers and cook for another 5 minutes. Add the paprika, stir for 20 seconds, and then the wine—you don't want the paprika to stick or burn.

Get a knife and cut off chunks of potato that are about ¾in thick. Please don't slice the potatoes! Cutting them up this way helps it to thicken the sauce.

Add the potatoes to the pan and cover with the stock. Add salt to taste. Cook until the potatoes are really tender, almost mushy, and the sauce has started to thicken. Add the fish, which will take only 2 or 3 minutes to cook through. Serve immediately.

CLAMS WITH SHERRY

This dish has a wonderful combination of sweet, salty, and savory flavors. For me, clams always conjure up memories of sitting on the seafront in Cádiz with my uncles and cousins. I remember being jealous as a child, because I was allowed to have a big bowl of clams, but not a glass of wine.

Please remember that clams, like mussels, must be totally fresh when you buy them; don't use frozen ones, and throw away any whose shells are open. Clams are usually sold in clean (tap) water, but I like to put them into salted water for an hour before cooking them, just to make doubly sure that there is no sand inside the shells. After that, I place them in more tap water for 20 minutes—to rid the clams of saltiness. This is a bit of a bother, but definitely worth it.

Serves 4

3 tablespoons extra virgin
   olive oil
1 large shallot, finely chopped
2 garlic cloves, finely chopped
1¾lb clams
¾ cup dry sherry,
   preferably Fino
1 thyme sprig
freshly ground black pepper
6oz Serrano ham, diced
handful of flat-leaf parsley,
   chopped

Pour the oil into a lidded saucepan that's large enough for the clams to fit easily in a single layer on the bottom as well as house the clams once they're open.

Sauté the shallot and garlic in the olive oil over low heat, making sure they don't brown. Next, add the clams and sherry and bring to a boil, to let some of the alcohol evaporate.

Add the thyme and pepper and cover with a tight-fitting lid. Leave the clams for 2 minutes. Check, and continue cooking if necessary—they will cook in less than 4 minutes. As soon as most of them are open, take the pan off the heat. Discard any clams that have remained shut.

Add the ham and the parsley and serve immediately.

RAZOR CLAMS WITH CHORIZO

The first time I cooked this recipe was with David Eyre (and a glass of Albariño), and we loved it so much that it was on the menu that very evening.

The razor clams must be alive and cleaned (ask your fishmonger to do this)—they live buried in the sand, and it's no fun munching on grit.

For an extra special finish to this dish, drizzle some mint-flavored olive oil over the top, the recipe for which is described on page 192.

Serves 4

2½ tablespoons extra virgin olive oil

7oz fresh chorizo, chopped

1¼lb small razor clams, cleaned

salt and freshly ground black pepper

Heat ½ tablespoon olive oil in a frying pan and sauté the chorizo over medium heat until the meat starts to turn a little brown and crisp—this will take about 6 minutes. Drain the fat off the chorizo and set the sausage aside.

In a sauté pan large enough to accommodate all the clams, heat the remaining olive oil and add the clams. Cover the pan with a tight-fitting lid for 3 to 4 minutes while the clams cook and steam.

Once the shells open, pour the clams into a big bowl, season with salt and pepper, then scatter the diced chorizo over the top. Discard any clams that don't open. Eat immediately.

BAKED SCALLOPS WITH CRISPY SERRANO HAM

The scallop shell is the symbol of Saint Santiago de Compostela, a popular destination for Christian pilgrims, and as a child I never knew that the contents could taste so good—I thought it was simply a religious symbol. The first time I ate scallops it was love at first taste of the beautiful shiny coral.

This dish is a great combination of flavors, with a hint of chile. Ask your fishmonger to clean the scallops for you, and to give you the shells, if available.

Serves 4

8 tablespoons extra virgin olive oil

8 slices of Serrano ham

8 scallops, with their shells (if available)

sea salt

1 garlic clove, finely chopped

5 sprigs of flat-leaf parsley, finely chopped

½ red chile, finely diced

1 tablespoon lemon juice

Preheat the oven to 425°F.

Heat 6 tablespoons olive oil in a small frying pan over medium-high heat. Cook the ham until it's crispy. Set the slices aside on paper towels to drain off any excess oil.

Mix together all the ingredients (including the remaining oil), except the ham. Put the scallops in their shells on a baking sheet. Distribute the parsley mixture between the scallops. You don't need much, otherwise you'll overwhelm the flavor of the shellfish. Bake for 8 minutes.

Place a slice of ham over each scallop and serve immediately with fresh bread to mop up the delicious juices.

GRILLED SQUID WITH AÏOLI

In Spain, the most popular way to cook squid is to cut up the body into rings, which are then battered and deep-fried. I have fond memories of my time in Madrid when I would party until the early hours and finish my festivities with a snack of *churros* (doughnuts), or with a mug of ultra-sweet and sticky hot chocolate. Then, later that morning I'd breakfast on a huge sandwich stuffed with crusty hoops of squid, washed down with a beer. Carbohydrate heaven. This recipe is altogether more elegant. Choose medium-size, white squid. Ask the fishmonger to prepare the squid for you (i.e., remove the beak and clean them).

Serves 4

2lb squid, ready prepared
1 small garlic clove, finely
    chopped
1 small red chile, seeds
    removed and finely chopped
juice of ½ lemon
⅔ cup extra virgin olive oil
5 flat-leaf parsley sprigs,
    chopped
salt and freshly ground
    black pepper
4 slices of white sourdough
    bread
4 mint sprigs

aïoli
2 large free-range egg yolks
    (at room temperature)
1 small garlic clove, finely
    chopped
1 teaspoon lemon juice
¼ teaspoon fine salt
⅔ cup extra virgin olive oil

Cut each squid body lengthwise and open it out flat. Score the inside of the squid diagonally from left to right and right to left to create a diamond-shape grid. This helps to keep the squid tender when you cook it. Leave the tentacles whole—I think it looks better.

Marinate the squid with the garlic, chile, lemon juice, olive oil, and parsley for 12 hours in the fridge.

Meanwhile, make the aïoli. Make sure that your egg yolks are at room temperature. Place them in a stainless steel mixing bowl along with the garlic, lemon juice, and salt. Whisk them together and then, very gradually, drizzle the olive oil into the mixture, continuing to whisk as you do so. You'll end up with a glistening sauce with a similar consistency to soft butter. Cover and refrigerate until needed.

In Spain we use a smooth cast-iron plate (or *plancha*) to grill things like squid. But there's no need to buy one, just heat your largest and heaviest frying pan until it's really hot. Season the squid with salt and pepper and grill the pieces for 2 minutes on each side—you want them to be a beautiful toasted color.

Toast the bread. Cut each slice of toast diagonally in half and then place one half on top of the other half off-center, so you have space to arrange the squid in a decorative pile over both slices. Finish with a spoonful of aïoli and a sprig of mint and serve.

GARLIC PRAWNS

This is a popular tapas, not only in Spain but also in our restaurants. It's incredibly simple to prepare and the secret is to use raw prawns (or large shrimp), so you don't overcook them, and also use good-quality olive oil. You can also grill these prawns—keep the shells on and cook all the other ingredients in a frying pan and serve as a dipping sauce for the prawns.

Serves 4 as an appetizer
6 tablespoons extra virgin
   olive oil
10 garlic cloves, chopped
20 raw prawns (or large
   shrimp), shelled
1 dried chile, crumbled
5 flat-leaf parsley sprigs
sea salt flakes

Heat the oil in a wok over high heat and add the chopped garlic. Give it a good stir and, before the garlic starts to color, add the prawns. When these begin to turn pink (which means they're cooked), after about 1 minute, turn them over. Add the chile and cook for another minute until the prawns are completely pink all over.

Coarsely chop the parsley, stir it in, then scatter some sea salt flakes over the top. Eat immediately with lots of bread to mop up the delicious juices.

OXTAIL STEW

Oxtail is gorgeous: the flavor is so intense thanks to all that fly-swishing exercise and the high ratio of bone to meat. This dish is popular all over Spain and it is traditionally served in restaurants located near bullrings.

Bullfighting is viewed with revulsion by lots of Spaniards, but it remains a popular pastime, particularly in rural areas. Bigger towns have permanent bullrings, but in my village—as in thousands of others—a bullring is set up just for special occasions. In the case of our village, the annual *corrida de toros* forms part of the celebrations for our riverside Virgin Mary in September: the focus of the event is the transportation of the Virgin Mary's statue from the chapel on the banks of the Tajo to the church in the middle of the village: the women take turns shouldering the dais as they walk the 2½ miles of rough dirt road. Once at the church, the Virgin joins in, metaphorically speaking, as an observer of the festivities.

Forty years ago, one of the village squares used to be blocked off as a makeshift bullring, and there were no professional matadors among us, just some young local men trying their hand at being matadors or *banderilleros*. Even now, although there is a visiting matador, young men are still eager to demonstrate their machismo. It's not something I ever wanted to do, although I kind of enjoyed the tension of watching people do really dangerous, silly things.

The village lays out a communal supper as part of the September celebrations, and of course the centerpiece is a huge beef casserole and limitless quantities of wine. My best friend's mother, Dioni, is responsible for the catering: four bulls are needed to feed around 2,000 revelers. She makes a *sofrito* of onion, which she then adds to the beef, along with nutmeg, black pepper, and a tanker load of white wine. The stew is boiled for about 5 hours over wood fires before it's ready. Dessert is fresh melon.

You won't need a slaughtered bull for this oxtail stew, but get your butcher to joint the oxtail between every vertebra. While the casserole is delicious under any circumstances, it undoubtedly tastes best if you cook it the day before you want to eat it... but remember that you need to marinate the oxtail for 24 hours too, so ideally start it two days before you want to eat it!

Serves 4
4½lb oxtail joints

marinade
1 quart red wine
5 medium carrots, diced
4 garlic cloves, quartered
1 large onion, diced
1 large leek, sliced
2 bay leaves
4 cloves
½ cinnamon stick

stew
salt and freshly ground
   black pepper
4 tablespoons extra virgin
   olive oil
2 cups beef stock
5 flat-leaf parsley sprigs,
   chopped
1 cup toasted
   almond slivers

Pat the oxtail joints dry and put them in a plastic bowl along with the marinade ingredients. Cover and put into the fridge for 24 hours.

The next day, drain and reserve the wine, then separate the vegetables from the meat. Season the oxtail with salt and pepper.

Heat the oil in a deep, heavy pot and brown the oxtail on all sides. At the end of this process there'll be burnt meaty bits on the bottom of the pan; these do not matter—just remove any excess oil, add the marinated vegetables, and cook them over medium heat. You'll find the vegetables lift the sticky bits from the pan. Sauté, stirring regularly, for about 20 minutes.

Now add the wine from the marinade and let the alcohol evaporate (this will take about 5 minutes), before returning the oxtail joints to the pan. Add the stock, cover, and simmer slowly for a minimum of 2, preferably 3, hours. Remove any foam that comes to the surface.

Spoon the stew onto plates, scattering some parsley and toasted almonds over each serving. Mop up the delicious juices with fresh, crusty bread.

SMOKED BEEF WITH FRISÉE AND POMEGRANATE SALAD

Cecina—smoked beef—is a speciality of León, a region in northern Spain. There, they cure the beef in salt, after which it is air-dried and then hot-smoked. In the US, you can usually buy locally smoked beef from deli counters and speciality shops, but you could also use bresaola, the Italian version.

This dish is so simple it's hardly a recipe! It is lovely to look at, though, and just the thing for a simple lunch on a crisp, sunny day in autumn. It is also good with grilled fish.

Serves 4 as an appetizer

7oz smoked beef, sliced
freshly ground black pepper
½ pomegranate
4 tablespoons extra virgin
  olive oil
2 tablespoons Moscatel white
  wine vinegar
½ garlic clove, very finely
  chopped
generous handful of frisée
  leaves

Arrange the beef slices on a plate and grind some fresh black pepper over the top.

Break up the pomegranate and pick out the seeds. Mix these with the oil, vinegar, and garlic to create a dressing. Toss the frisée leaves in the dressing, then arrange the salad around and on top of the beef.

MEATBALLS WITH ONION SAUCE

Albóndigas, or meatballs, are hugely popular all over Spain, and the favorite way of making them is with tomato sauce. But my dad loves them with onion sauce, so that's the way we always have them. My variation on my mother's recipe is the addition of blue cheese to the meatballs.

Serves 4
(makes about
24 meatballs)

meatballs

¾lb ground beef

¾lb ground pork

1 garlic clove, finely chopped

2 large free-range eggs, beaten

¼ cup dry white wine

salt and freshly ground black pepper

5 flat-leaf parsley sprigs, chopped

3½oz blue cheese, such as Gorgonzola or Stilton

½ cup flour, for dusting

extra virgin olive oil, for frying

onion sauce

1 medium onion, finely diced

2 tablespoons extra virgin olive oil

1 teaspoon plain flour

2½ cups chicken stock, warmed

5 flat-leaf parsley sprigs, chopped

¼ cup toasted almond slivers

Mix together the meats, garlic, eggs, wine, salt and pepper, and parsley. The easiest way to do this is with your hands—really squish everything together thoroughly. Set the mixture aside in the fridge for a couple of hours to allow the flavors to develop. Make golf ball size pieces of the mixture—about 1oz—and roll them into a neat ball: you should make about 24.

Break the cheese up into small nuggets. Take a meatball in one hand, and with your other hand use your thumb to make a hole in the meatball. Add a piece of cheese and close up the hole by pinching the meat mixture together. Roll the meatball again and make sure the cheese is fully covered in the meat. Repeat until all the meatballs have a piece of cheese in the middle. Next, roll the meatballs in the flour.

Pour enough olive oil into a medium-sized frying pan or wok to come halfway up the meatballs once they are added. Heat the oil over medium heat and once it is hot, cook the meatballs in batches, about 5 or 6 at a time. Allow 1 minute on each side. Drain them on paper towels and keep warm.

To make the onion sauce, sauté the onion in the olive oil until soft but not colored. This will take about 5 minutes. Add the flour, stir, and cook for another minute, before adding the warm stock. Season with salt and pepper, stir well, and simmer for about 10 minutes. Remove any froth that comes to the surface. Blend the sauce with a hand blender to give it a smooth consistency. Bring the sauce back to a simmer, add the meatballs, and cook for another minute.

Divide the meatballs and sauce between four warmed bowls, scatter the almonds and parsley over the top, and eat immediately.

BEEF SLICES COOKED WITH SHERRY

My dad has retired from farming dairy cows, but my older brother, Antonio, keeps Limousin beef cattle—a breed well known for its sturdiness, good health, and excellent eating. Antonio loves driving anything with two or four wheels, so his preferred way of rounding up the cattle is with a 4-wheeler.

This is a very good midweek supper dish that is ready in less than 10 minutes. Sirloin or rump steak is ideal, but sliced beef scallops will also do. This is a new (and cheaper) cut from just below the rump.

Serves 4

4 slices beef steak, approx.
   7oz each
salt and freshly ground
   black pepper
2 tablespoons extra virgin
   olive oil
1 garlic clove, finely diced
1 rosemary sprig
1 (10oz) jar piquillo peppers,
   drained and sliced
6 tablespoons dry sherry
4 flat-leaf parsley sprigs,
   chopped
4 mint sprigs, chopped
1 head romaine, sliced
extra virgin olive oil

Slice the steaks into ½in-wide strips and season with salt and pepper.

Heat the oil in a non-stick frying pan or wok over high heat until it shimmers. Add the garlic, beef, and rosemary and stir-fry for about 1 minute. When the meat starts to turn a bit brown, add the pepper slices. Cook for 1 minute more and then pour in the sherry. Let it bubble furiously until the alcohol has evaporated—about 2 minutes. Remove from the heat and stir in the chopped parsley and mint. Season to taste with salt and pepper.

Divide up the lettuce between four plates, followed by the beef mixture, making sure each serving gets some of the juices. Shake a few drops of extra virgin olive oil over the beef, and serve with a glass of sherry or white wine.

FILLET STEAK ON TOAST WITH CARAMELIZED ONIONS AND MELTED CHEESE

This recipe first appeared in the English version of the cookbook, *1,080 Recipes*. It's a Spanish institution, a culinary bible you'll find in most Spanish homes, and I was incredibly flattered to be asked to contribute!

The recipe is a result of playing with the memories and flavors from my childhood. I remember being scared of the unwashed and silent farmers who used to come to the door in early summer selling Torta de Barros cheese—which was sealed in boxes to contain the fetid-feet stench. It's an unpasteurized, soft sheep cheese with a smell that belies its mild, savory taste. The traditional way of eating it is for the entire family to sit around the cheese on a balmy evening, cut off the top, and dig out the gooey cheese with a spoon. Piled on top of toasted country bread and washed down with a strong red wine, it makes for a great alfresco meal. Cheeseburgers are fast food all over the world, but they don't have a soul: they are the opposite of everything that Spanish cooking is about. But while not classically Spanish, beef and cheese is undoubtedly a great combination. So, I decided to take the basic ingredients and make a dish to savor. I used the most tender, chargrilled beef, the most sublime cheese (it is, honestly), and meltingly sweet, caramelized onions. The secret is extra virgin olive oil and slow, slow cooking—for an hour or so. Sadly, Torta de Barros cheese is difficult to track down, so I recommend Camembert with the rind removed as a substitute.

Serves 4

caramelized onions
6 tablespoons extra virgin
  olive oil
5 medium onions, finely sliced
1 teaspoon superfine sugar
1 small bay leaf

steak sandwiches
4 fillet steaks, 7oz each
7oz Camembert
1 tablespoon extra virgin
  olive oil
salt and freshly ground
  black pepper
4 slices of sourdough bread
2 oregano sprigs, leaves
  stripped

First, caramelize the onions: heat the olive oil in a heavy-bottomed sauté pan over low heat, then add the onions, sugar, and bay leaf. Give everything a good stir, cover with a lid, and slowly cook the onions until they are a deep nut-brown in color; stir occasionally. This process will take longer than you think—about an hour.

Meanwhile, bring the steaks to room temperature (this will take about 20 to 30 minutes); de-rind the cheese and divide it into four chunky slices.

Toward the end of the onions' cooking time, heat a non-stick frying pan over high heat. Add the oil and, when it's shimmering, gently place a steak into the pan. You should fry the steaks one at a time: if you add all four at once they'll steam rather than fry. For rare steaks about 1in thick, cook for 1–2 minutes on each side, and rest for 5 minutes.

Season each steak with salt and pepper, place a cheese slice on top of it, and set aside in a warm place so that the cheese begins to melt. Meanwhile, toast the bread.

Spoon the caramelized onions onto the toast, place the cheese-smothered steaks on top, finish with a sprinkle of oregano leaves, and serve immediately.

RICE

In my family, paella is viewed in a similar way to how American families view an outdoor barbecue—only when the weather is sunny is the equipment dusted off. What is more, the whole family should be together—for me, this is usually on vacation down in Cádiz; and then the final criterion is that we've got the time and inclination to prepare the myriad ingredients. In other words, we enjoy paella once or twice a year.

Paella is a "dry rice" dish and, truth be told, we prefer soupy or "wet rice" dishes known as *arroz caldoso*. Just as paella refers to the pan in which the rice is cooked, *caldoso* means that the rice has been cooked in a *caldero*—literally a cauldron; for 21st-century purposes, that means a deep soup pot or cast-iron casserole.

I like to cook paella for lots of people; *caldosos* are more soupy, everyday creations, but are just as delicious. The key thing for either style is the rice: wet or dry, Spanish rice recipes are all based around simmering the grains in flavorful liquid, whether that's fish or chicken stock or sweetened milk. Cooks through the centuries have capitalized on the wonderful sponge-like ability of the grains which, when cooked, still retain a bite and a loose, non-sticky texture.

RICE VARIETIES AND GROWING REGIONS

And we Spanish love our rice. Wherever there are wetlands or rivers—mostly on the Mediterranean side of Spain—you'll find rice being grown: from small municipalities such as Sa Pobla in Mallorca or Pals in Girona (where all the rice is eaten locally), to

the other end of the scale in Andalucía and Extremadura, where large areas are under cultivation and the focus is on growing long-grain rice for export to the rest of Europe.

The rice that you need for cooking Spanish rice dishes is the short- to medium-grain variety, the most famous of which is Bomba. An old-fashioned, low-yield rice, Bomba is relatively difficult to grow and so is much more expensive than other short- to medium-grain varieties. However, it is a popular choice for paella novices, as it is more tolerant of a couple of extra minutes' cooking, and the grains don't stick together as easily.

Bomba is well-known all over Spain so sells easily under its own name. Most other rice varieties, however, are newer and have really unsexy names such as Balilla x Sollana and Sequial, so these tend to be marketed under the name of one of the three rice *Denominaciones de Origen* (DOs), where they (as well as Bomba) are grown—namely Calasparra, the Ebro Delta, and Valencia.

My favorite rice comes from Calasparra, in the mountains of Murcia in southeast Spain. It is a beautiful region and the only place in Spain where rice is grown above sea level.

The cooler climate and carefully controlled, cold river water means that the rice crop takes longer to ripen, so it has loads of flavor.

Paella aficionados are fond of medium-grain Bahía and Senia from the Valencia DO; it means that they are a whiz at making paella, as these types of rice can overcook easily.

OTHER RICE VARIETIES

People often ask me what sort of rice to use when Spanish rice varieties aren't available in their shops. No other type of rice exactly matches the characteristics of Spanish short- and medium-grain rice, so I usually tell people to keep asking their deli or supermarket to stock it.

As for substitutes, look for Italian Carnaroli and Vialone Nano rice, traditionally used for making risotto; Carnaroli, in particular, holds its shape and absorbs broth well, making it acceptable for paella. Arborio, another risotto rice, produces a softer, creamier finish, so it is better suited to soupy rice dishes. You will, of course, have to adjust the cooking times, and try not to stir the rice too much.

The starch in long-grain, perfumed rice such as Basmati has a slightly different structure and it doesn't absorb as much liquid as rounder varieties; the end result is almost fluffy. It's lovely but shouldn't be your first choice. As for "easy cook" and blanched rice, please ignore them completely as they barely absorb anything.

ESPERANZA'S PAELLA

Esperanza Añonuevo is a good friend and also a chef. She comes from a tiny village called Requena in the mountains about an hour away from the city of Valencia, and she is an excellent person to share her experience on how to make great paella.

Esperanza's father is a farmer who grows grapes for the local wine cooperative. She is one of eight children. They are all now grown up, but they still—with their own families—go back home to their mother for Sunday lunch. So every week she cooks paella for about thirty people.

Paella is a year-round dish, but the ingredients change seasonally. In autumn, it will probably include mushrooms; in winter, turnips, pork ribs, and sausages could be added; spring will see vegetables such as asparagus and artichokes included; and in summer, especially during July and August, snails are a favorite.

Paella is all about making the most of the ingredients that are readily available. The thing to remember is that paella originated as a farm workers' lunch. It should be simple, robustly flavored, and cooked over an open fire. Esperanza's family uses vine trimmings for kindling, the aromatic smoke subtly flavoring the rice. Even more important than the meat and vegetables is the stock; if you don't have homemade, flavorful stock, think of something else to make.

The other thing to mention is that if you are going to make paella with any degree of regularity, it is worth buying a paella pan. The trick behind achieving rice that has absorbed all the stock, but hasn't overcooked, is to make sure that all the rice cooks evenly. To do this, the rice has to be spread in a thin layer over a pan that is capable of transmitting heat evenly across its entire base.

For lots of first timers, making sure that the rice cooks properly is a slightly scary prospect. Esperanza, of course, thinks it is easy. If the rice has cooked but there is still liquid (i.e., you added too much stock in the first place), spoon off the excess. Conversely, if the paella has simmered dry but the rice isn't ready, you can always add more stock. So, if you are a paella novice, have a small pan of boiling stock ready toward the end of the cooking time.

Esperanza's paella includes several varieties of fresh beans special to the Valencia area: firstly, the *garrofó*, which is like a fava bean; then, a small white bean called *tavella*, akin to a fresh green bean; and lastly, a flat green bean called *ferraúra*, which is similar to the Italian flat bean available in the US.

Serves 6

1lb chicken, jointed into
  approx. 6 pieces
1lb rabbit, jointed into
  approx. 6 pieces
salt and freshly ground
  black pepper
4 tablespoons extra virgin
  olive oil
2 garlic cloves, sliced
2 ripe tomatoes, chopped
2 teaspoons spanish smoked
  paprika (mild)
7oz fava beans
7oz thin green beans
  (or omit and double the
  quantity of flat beans)
7oz flat green beans, sliced
  into 1½in lengths
1½ quarts chicken stock,
  warmed
1 pinch saffron (approx.
  20 threads), soaked in
  2 tablespoons hot water
2 cups paella rice, such as
  Calasparra

Season the chicken and rabbit with salt. Take a large frying pan, or an 18in paella pan, and heat the oil over medium heat. Cook the meat for 7 minutes, or until the pieces are browned all over.

Reduce the heat and add the garlic and tomatoes to the pan, then stir in the paprika—adding the spice last improves the flavor of the tomatoes. Sauté for 2 minutes before adding the various types of beans. Season with salt and pepper.

Pour in the stock, bring everything to a simmer, and let cook for 10 minutes or so. Add the saffron water, give it a good stir, then turn the heat up to high and scatter the rice across the whole of the pan. (Esperanza says local cooks sometimes pour in the rice in the sign of a cross; we don't think this is necessary.) Stir the rice to make sure it is evenly distributed, and then leave it uncovered for 10 minutes.

After 10 minutes, reduce the heat to low and cook for another 8 minutes until the rice is *al punto*, or still has a little bite to it.

Remove the paella from the heat and cover with paper towels or a kitchen towel. Let it rest for 5 minutes before serving.

SEAFOOD PAELLA

This is the paella that everyone makes all over Spain. You'll see people on a Sunday in picnic parks, cooking this paella, or a version of it, on their grills.

Use a mixture of firm-fleshed white fish—select the freshest you can find; here I have used monkfish.

Serves 6

6 tablespoons extra virgin olive oil
1lb locally sourced monkfish, cubed
2 small onions, diced
2 garlic cloves, sliced
3 ripe tomatoes chopped, or 14oz can chopped tomatoes
½ cup white wine
2 teaspoons spanish smoked paprika (mild)
salt and freshly ground black pepper
10oz squid, ready cleaned and sliced
3½ to 4 cups chicken or fish stock, warmed
pinch of saffron, about 30 threads, soaked in 2 tablespoons hot water
2 cups paella rice, such as Calasparra
12 raw shrimp
1 cup peas
10oz mussels
12oz clams
5 flat-leaf parsley sprigs, chopped
6 lemon slices

Heat the olive oil in a very large frying pan or, ideally, a paella pan that's roughly 18in in diameter. Cook the monkfish over medium heat until browned—this will take about 3 minutes. Remove and set aside in a warm place while you prepare the *sofrito*, or onion mixture, in the same pan.

Cook the onions and garlic for 5 minutes until soft, then add the tomatoes and the wine; let reduce a little for another 5 minutes, then stir in the paprika. Season with salt and pepper.

Add the squid and give everything a good stir. Stir in 3½ cups stock and saffron water, turn the heat up to high, and bring the liquid to a boil. Pour in the rice, give another good stir, and then add the monkfish and stir once. Cook uncovered over high heat for 10 minutes. Do not stir again—this is not a risotto.

Add the shrimp, followed by the peas, and lastly the shellfish. Cover with foil, reduce the heat to low, and cook for another 8 minutes. Remember that the shellfish will release their own juices, so you probably won't need to add extra stock toward the end, but if you think the rice is looking dry, add a ladle more.

Remove from the heat, remove the foil from the rice, and replace with some paper towels or a kitchen towel; let sit for 5 minutes to allow the paella to breathe.

Scatter the parsley over the rice, arrange the lemon slices, then put the paella into the middle of the table and let everyone help themselves. You may find there is some crusty, slightly caramelized rice on the base of the pan; this is called the *socarrat* and is the sign of a well-cooked paella.

HARE WITH RICE

This is my mother's recipe, *arroz con liebre*, and it's a good example of a soupy rice dish using easily available ingredients. Hares were once really common in the Cáceres countryside where my family lives. In fact, hares were so common they were considered a pest. Nowadays, I think myself lucky if I see one. Consequently, my mother very rarely makes this *arroz*, which is a pity as it is simple and delicious.

In the US, hare is sometimes hard to find since it is not widely cooked. A butcher that specializes in poultry or game, however, should be able to supply one.

If you cannot find whole dried sweet (*choricero*) peppers in your local deli or supermarket, use two teaspoons of smoked sweet paprika instead, and add it once the onions and garlic have cooked.

Serves 4

1 small hare, jointed into
  12 to 15 pieces
salt and freshly ground
  black pepper
4 tablespoons extra virgin
  olive oil
1 medium onion, finely sliced
2 garlic cloves, finely sliced
6 tablespoons dry white wine
1 quart chicken stock, warmed
1 bay leaf
1 dried choricero pepper
1¼ cups rice, such as
  Calasparra
handful of chopped flat-
  leaf parsley

Season the hare with salt and pepper. Heat the olive oil in a sauté pan and brown the meat. Set the pieces to one side while you cook the onion and garlic in the same pan. Add the onion and garlic and, once they are soft and slightly colored, pour in the wine and give everything a good stir, scraping up any bits from the base of the pan. Put the meat back in the pan, then add the chicken stock, bay leaf, and the *choricero* pepper. Bring everything to a boil and simmer, covered, for 30 minutes or longer—it depends on how old the hare was.

Add the rice and simmer, covered, for another 20 minutes until the rice is cooked (but still has a slight bite to it).

Ladle into four warmed soup bowls, adding a scattering of chopped parsley over each serving.

SOUPY RICE WITH MUSHROOMS AND LANGOUSTINES

If you've never made paella because it sounds a bit complicated, this *arroz caldoso* or soupy rice is for you—it's very easy to do and tastes fantastic.

It is an adaptation of a *caldoso* that I came across in Catalonia, which featured lobster, the local fresh pork sausages called *butifarra*, and saffron milk cap mushrooms, which are a pretty yellow color and have a dense flesh. If you can find these ingredients that's great! But if you're heading to your local stores and not Barcelona, just be sure to source the best plain pork sausages (no herbs or spices please); really good-quality stock; and meaty mushrooms. If you cannot find Spanish paella rice, use risotto rice instead.

Serves 4

5 tablespoons extra virgin olive oil

2 large garlic cloves, chopped

14oz can chopped tomatoes

7oz field mushrooms

4 large free-range pork sausages

1¼ cups rice (preferably Calasparra)

6 tablespoons dry white wine

1 quart chicken or fish stock, warmed

sea salt

8 raw langoustines or prawns, unshelled

handful of chopped flat-leaf parsley,

Heat the oil in a big pan or casserole over medium to high heat. Cook the garlic for about 3 minutes, until it turns golden, then add the tomatoes and cook until the juices have reduced.

If you are using large, flat-capped field mushrooms, take a teaspoon and scrape out the brown gills—they will color the rice and make it look unappetizing. Pink-gilled mushrooms don't need this treatment. Slice the mushrooms caps and stalks into ¾in slices. Cut the sausages into ¾in slices.

Stir in the mushrooms and sausage slices and cook the mixture for another 3 minutes. Turn up the heat and add the rice, giving everything a good stir, then pour in the wine. The mixture will bubble nicely; let the alcohol evaporate before adding the stock.

Season with salt to taste, give everything another stir, then turn the heat down. Let simmer gently until the rice is cooked, about 18 to 20 minutes.

When the rice looks very nearly done, add the langoustines. They'll take about 5 minutes to cook, but remember they will continue to cook in the rice even after the pan has been taken off the heat.

Scatter the parsley over the rice and serve immediately.

SAFFRON

Saffron, or *azafrán*, as it's called in Spanish, is definitely one of those "less is more" spices. Its rusty, honey aroma and warm, slightly bitter taste can topple over into an astringent, almost medicinal quality. If a cook has been overly generous with the quantities, it reminds of me of old-fashioned hospitals and iodine dressings. In other words, it's not very nice at all!

Saffron, or rather the saffron crocus, is grown in several countries, but in Spain we firmly believe that we grow the best. The saffron fields of La Mancha are a glorious sight in October: acres and rows of lilac and amethyst flowers glowing in the yellow autumn sunshine.

Harvesting the flowers has to be done by hand, and it's a family affair: workers in Madrid return home and help with the picking. It is only the red stigmas in the middle of the flower, not the petals, that are dried to make the spice, so an area the size of a football field is needed to yield just 1lb of the finished product.

The pickers work their way down the rows, expertly plucking flowers and popping them into open-weave wicker baskets, designed to let the air circulate around the precious contents. Once the stigmas have been removed, they're roasted for 30 minutes over low flame in a cloth-lined basket; too much heat and the filaments will scorch, too little and the moisture will encourage mold and spoil the saffron. The roasting process, which gives the saffron a better aroma and color, is peculiar to Spanish saffron.

People always go on about how saffron is the most expensive spice in the world, which is true; but it's sold in very small quantities—less than ¼oz—which is enough for about ten family-sized paellas. It's a spice for special occasions and, frankly, even if you had all the money in the world, you wouldn't want to savor it on a daily basis. It's the other end of the usage spectrum to black pepper, so don't think about the price tag—just concern yourself with the quality.

Good-quality saffron has an intense, crimson-rust color—if there are white or yellow threads in it, these are the crocus styles (also in the middle bit of the flower), which don't have any flavor. The other thing to look out for—although you can test this out only after you have purchased the saffron—is that the filaments are crisp to touch: this indicates that the stigmas have been dried properly. If you buy saffron from producers who belong to the *Azafrán de la Mancha Denominación de Origen*, then these quality control checks will have been done for you.

Lastly, remember to use saffron from the current year's harvest; like all spices, the fragrance fades with time.

SAFFRON ICE CREAM

In this ice cream, the saffron provides an interesting background flavor to the rich egginess of the custard. It goes really well with pears poached in Rioja wine. Or, try it with a gooey chocolate brownie. If you don't have an ice-cream maker, stir the mixture every 20 minutes while it is freezing, until it is a creamy consistency.

Serves 4
12 saffron threads
1¼ cups whole milk
1¼ cups heavy cream
4 large free-range egg yolks
½ cup superfine sugar

First, make a creamy infusion with the saffron: put 12 threads (certainly no more) into a non-stick saucepan with the milk and cream. Bring the mixture to a boil and turn it off immediately. Leave to infuse for 1 hour.

In another saucepan, beat the eggs and sugar together. Strain the saffron milk into the egg mixture, stirring as you pour. Place this mixture over medium heat and stir continuously until it thickens to a custard that coats the back of a wooden spoon.

Leave the custard to cool and then freeze it following your ice-cream maker manufacturer's instructions.

PEARS POACHED IN RIOJA

Please don't be tempted to put a cheap red wine into this recipe—it will show in the final dish. This is a classic dessert all over Spain; my variation is to put cloves and black pepper into the red wine sauce. Choose similar-sized fruit that are not quite ripe and still firm.

Serves 4
4 Conference pears
2 tablespoons lemon juice
1 bottle Rioja wine, or other good-quality red
peel of ½ lemon and ½ orange, pith removed
4 tablespoons superfine sugar
1 cinnamon stick
1 clove
3 black peppercorns

Peel the pears and roll them in the lemon juice to keep them from discoloring.

Place all the other ingredients in a saucepan and simmer gently for anything from 30 to 50 minutes—it will depend on your pears. You want the fruit to stay a bit firm, so prod them occasionally after 20 minutes cooking. Allow it to cool in the wine.

Remove the pears from the wine and set aside. Remove the peel, cinnamon, and other spices and discard. Place the saucepan over low heat and reduce the wine until it thinly coats the back of a spoon. This will take about 10 minutes.

Halve each pear lengthwise, removing the core and seeds, then cut into segments, but not all the way through to the base of the fruit. Arrange each pear into a fan on the plate then add a spoonful of saffron ice cream. Ladle the wine sauce over everything.

SPANISH APPLE PIE

This version of a classic dessert popular in the Basque Country is the invention of my friend and fellow chef Rafael. There are several components to this pie and it's a good idea to make the crust the day before you want to eat it to allow the flavors to develop.

Serves 6 to 8

crust
4 tablespoons butter
½ cup superfine sugar
¼ cup ground almonds
¾ teaspoon baking powder
1¼ cups flour
1 vanilla pod, split lengthwise
1 large free-range egg yolk, beaten
2 tablespoons good-quality dark rum

apple filling
1lb apples, such as Granny Smith or McIntosh (cubed and peeled weight)
¼ cup superfine sugar
1 vanilla pod

vanilla pastry cream
3 large free-range egg yolks
¼ cup cornstarch
⅓ cup superfine sugar
2 cups whole milk
1 vanilla pod

First, make the crust. Combine the butter and the sugar in a mixing bowl until smooth and pale. Mix together the ground almonds, baking powder, and flour, and then slowly add these to the butter mixture. Keep beating until the mixture looks like sand.

Scrape the seeds from the vanilla pod, then add these to the bowl along with the egg yolk and rum; work the dough just enough to blend everything together. Wrap in plastic wrap and set aside to relax in the fridge for at least 12 hours.

Just cover the apple cubes with water and stir in the superfine sugar and vanilla pod. Bring the water to a gentle simmer and poach the fruit until it is tender, which will take 5 to 7 minutes. Scoop out the cubes and set aside; reduce the liquid until it takes on a syrupy consistency—you will use this on the pastry crust.

Now make the vanilla cream. Mix together the egg yolks, cornstarch, and superfine sugar in a bowl. Bring the milk to a boil with the vanilla pod and gradually add this to the egg and sugar mixture (vanilla pod included).

Transfer the custard to a clean, non-stick saucepan and cook it for at least 5 minutes, stirring continuously. Once the custard has thickened (which you can judge from the slight spoon trails left in the sauce, or from whether the custard coats the back of the spoon), remove it from the heat and let cool. Remove the vanilla pod only when you are ready to assemble the pie

Preheat the oven to 325°F.

Spread the apple cubes in one layer over the base of a 9in pie or tart dish (or you can use a deep baking sheet for ease). Pour the custard over the top. Roll out the pastry to a thickness just less than ¼in and lay this over the custard. Use a toothpick to prick some holes into the pastry.

Bake for 30 minutes until a nice golden color. Brush some of the sugary apple syrup over the crust and let cool on the counter for about 5 minutes before serving.

WINTER

Brassicas ✳ **Olive Oil and Olives** ✳ **Legumes** ✳ **Chorizo** ✳ **La Matanza** ✳
Morcilla ✳ **Offal** ✳ **Ham and Pork** ✳ **Christmas** ✳ **Game and Poultry** ✳
Oranges and Quinces ✳ **Turrón**

It may be cold outside, but there are plenty of culinary delights to celebrate in the warmth of the Spanish kitchen: bitter Seville and blood oranges; the new season's olive oil; and, in rural areas, *La Matanza*, the annual dispatch of a pig to be turned into pork, ham, and sausages.

The hunting season opens in the autumn, but game dishes really come into their own in the depths of winter.

I love cooking game, both furred and feathered kinds, and even though most is now farmed and available all year round, I always like to wait until my suppliers arrive with the real thing. It has a far superior flavor.

The highlight, however, has to be Christmas; not for us an overgrown turkey, but my grandmother's partridge casserole. And some turrón to finish the meal.

SAUTÉED PURPLE-SPROUTING BROCCOLI

Spanish housewives don't like to waste anything, and the following recipe is a great way to use up any leftover broccoli—or any other green vegetable, such as spinach or green beans. We call this a *rehogado*, which basically means a previously boiled vegetable sautéed in olive oil with garlic or small bits of ham. It is not traditional to add smoked paprika, but I think it jazzes up the dish nicely. I know purple-sprouting broccoli is not very Spanish, but I love it anyway!

Serves 4 as a side dish
14oz purple-sprouting broccoli
sea salt
3 tablespoons extra virgin olive oil
1 garlic clove, finely sliced
½ teaspoon spanish smoked paprika (hot)
3 salted anchovies, chopped

Put the broccoli stems in a saucepan so they all lie in a single layer. Season with salt and add enough boiling water to just cover them, then boil vigorously for a couple of minutes until the stems are *al punto*—still a bit crunchy. Drain and put in a bowl of iced water to cool down.

Heat the oil in a frying pan over medium heat and cook the garlic until it just begins to turn golden. Add the broccoli and the paprika and give everything a good stir. Continue to cook the vegetables for another minute, stirring regularly to make sure that the stems are thoroughly coated in garlicky oil. Stir in the chopped anchovies and serve.

CAULIFLOWER WITH A SEVILLE ORANGE DRESSING

The cauliflower is not a vegetable from the New World. Along with broccoli (to which it is closely related), the cauliflower probably originated in Syria. The first mention of its cultivation in Spain dates from the twelfth century. Cauliflower is a strange vegetable—it's been available to chefs for a very long time and yet doesn't offer many ways in which to be cooked.

However, this is an outstanding warm salad, and is an excellent accompaniment to roast chicken; the simple dressing works equally well with broccoli. If you can't find Seville oranges or they are out of season, use sour Valencia oranges plus the juice of one lemon.

Serves 4 as a side dish
2 garlic cloves
1 teaspoon sea salt
4 tablespoons Seville orange juice
1 medium cauliflower
4 tablespoons extra virgin olive oil
small bunch of cilantro

Use a pestle and mortar to crush the garlic cloves and salt to make a thick paste. Scrape this into a large bowl and stir in the orange juice. Set aside for 30 minutes to let the flavors mingle.

Break the cauliflower up into florets—each about the size of a golf ball—and steam for 5 minutes, until cooked but still a bit crunchy. Transfer to a serving dish immediately, then fold through the orange and garlic dressing. Drizzle the olive oil over the top, then set aside to cool a little until warm.

Just before serving, coarsely tear the cilantro with your fingers, stir it in, and serve.

STIR-FRIED RED CABBAGE

I like the crunchiness of red cabbage with steamed fish. The important thing for this dish is to slice the cabbage as thinly as possible: a mandolin is ideal, otherwise make sure you have a very sharp, long-bladed knife on hand.

Serves 4 as a side dish

½ head red cabbage

3 tablespoons extra virgin
   olive oil

2 garlic cloves, chopped

3 tablespoons Cabernet
   red wine vinegar

salt and freshly ground
   black pepper

¼ cup pine nuts, toasted

Remove the stem of the cabbage, then place it cut-side down on the cutting board and slice carefully into very thin long shreds.

Heat the oil in a non-stick wok or frying pan over medium to high heat and add the garlic. You don't want it to turn brown, so cook for a maximum of 30 seconds before stirring in the cabbage. Continue to cook, stirring regularly, for 5 to 7 minutes.

Add the vinegar and continue to cook the cabbage until the vinegar has evaporated, which will take another 2 or 3 minutes. The cabbage will turn from purple to a lovely red color.

Season with salt and pepper, toss the cabbage, and serve with the pine nuts mixed in.

OLIVE OIL

I cannot imagine cooking without olive oil; when I say "olive oil," I mean extra virgin olive oil. I use it for everything, from salad dressings to cooking meat. It is difficult to decide which is my favorite, but I think oil made from the Arbequina olive is a good all-arounder. It is produced mainly in Catalonia and Mallorca, and it's neither too peppery nor too bitter, with a lovely almond sweetness.

Of course, there are other regions and other varieties: in fact, there are more than 260 olive varieties to be found in Spain, although only a fraction of these are used in oil production. Andalucía, for example, is well known for the Picual olive, which accounts for an amazing 20 percent of world production, and is another great all-arounder.

Whatever the variety or blend of extra virgin olive oil, always look for the term "cold pressed" on the label when buying it. This means that the olives have been simply squeezed—hard—to extract the oil, rather than pressed with the help of heat and water. The latter method is more efficient but it affects the flavor slightly.

Needless to say, cold-pressing olives is the old-fashioned way of doing things that my grandmother would recognize. In her day, the picked olives used to hang around in sacks outside her and other villagers' houses for several days, even a week or more, until a guy from the cooperative came around with a trailer to take them away. Ripe olives have a really strong smell, and if they aren't processed, their acidity levels rise, resulting in oil that really doesn't taste very nice. Nowadays, the olives are whisked off within a few hours of picking.

Most people of my grandmother's generation would take their containers to the local cooperative to fill up with olive oil when they needed it—something you can still do if you happen to be in rural Spain in the winter months.

My grandmother would be surprised at the modern habit of using one kind of oil to cook with, and another for use as a condiment, drizzled over soups and salads as a finishing touch. And I am no different. It feels totally natural to me to use the cold-pressed, extra virgin olive oil that I grew up with for everything, but I'm lucky that I can buy it in large enough quantities for it not to be a ridiculously expensive habit. Feel free to use a lighter (and cheaper) olive oil for cooking, but at the same time, please do not be too precious about using the extra virgin kind.

There are enough bottled, single estate, unfiltered, organic, and mono-varietal oils out there to keep you going for several lifetimes. My advice is to find one that you like (and can afford) and to use it whenever the mood strikes you, not just once in a blue moon. Remember that olive oil keeps its fresh flavor for only a year.

OLIVES FOR EATING

The tiny Arbequina olives don't just make excellent oil—they are also good for eating. But all sorts of varieties are turned into table olives. My family, for example, grows Cornezuelo and Manzanilla olive trees. The former is a variety local to Extremadura, a bit like the more famous Greek Kalamata, while the green Manzanilla is familiar to most of us, stuffed with a sliver of anchovy, pepper, or almond. It is one of my favorite olives.

Olive-picking in winter was a task I hated as a child—the whole family had to do it, even me, the youngest. My dad always said that I couldn't get out of it because I'd been too naughty at school. First, the olive trees had to beaten with sticks so that the olives would fall onto the nets spread below. The frost meant our fingers would be frozen after a few minutes of gathering them up off the ground.

My mother cures the olives herself. One by one, she cracks open the fruit with a tap of a mallet, then puts them into very salty water. This brine has to be changed every day for three weeks, by which stage the bitterness in the fruit will have disappeared. My mother then adds thyme, garlic, orange and lemon peels, black peppercorns, and whole dried red pepper. She does not like to add things like chile, which she feels can overwhelm the flavor of the olives. I like them to have a tingle, so I add a bit of chile to mine. It's impossible to buy fresh olives where I live in London, so I buy top-quality jarred plain Manzanilla olives and then marinate them my mother's way.

The other eating olive that I love is the Gordal variety from Seville in Andalucía; the olives are often bigger than quail eggs. My favorite way to prepare them is pitted and stuffed with a piece of fresh orange and then dressed in extra virgin olive oil. I then serve the olives with a scattering of sea salt, freshly ground black pepper, and dried oregano flowers. They're incredibly addictive and one of my most popular tapas. Here is the recipe.

3 oranges
14oz Gordal olives, pitted
3 tablespoons extra virgin
 olive oil
sea salt flakes
freshly ground black pepper
1 teaspoon dried oregano
 (preferably the flowers)

Peel the oranges, making sure that you remove all the pith. Take a very sharp knife and slice down either side of each segment, so that you remove it from the fruit, leaving behind the membrane. Now slice each segment in half and use to stuff the olives.

Dress the olives with the olive oil, sea salt, pepper, and lastly the dried oregano and serve.

ORANGE-MARINATED COD

This is gorgeous: it's a kind of do-it-yourself salt cod or a semi-cured cod carpaccio. You need to begin the cure a day before you want to eat the fish but, trust me, the advance planning is worth it.

Ask your fishmonger for a fillet from the tail of the cod—the flesh is not as thick, so the sugar/salt cure works better.

Serves 4

2¼ cups superfine sugar

2¼ cups fine salt

3 oranges

5 marjoram sprigs, leaves stripped

1lb cod fillet, from the tail

2 tablespoons extra virgin olive oil

1 tablespoon Moscatel white wine vinegar

freshly ground black pepper

1 tablespoon salted capers, rinsed

16 black olives, pitted and halved

½ red onion, very finely sliced

Mix the sugar, salt, the juice of 1 orange, and the leaves from 3 of the marjoram sprigs (roughly a tablespoon).

Spread the salt mixture on a non-reactive baking sheet or gratin dish in a smooth layer to cover the base. Place the cod fillet skin-side down onto the mixture, then pat the rest of the mixture on top of the fish to cover it completely. Cover with plastic wrap and leave in the fridge for 12 hours.

When it's ready, rinse the cod under cold running water then pat it dry. At this stage the cod can be left in the fridge for up to 4 days.

Slice the cod as thinly as possible and arrange the pieces on a serving platter.

Peel the remaining oranges and, using a very sharp knife, first remove all the pith, then slice vertically down the orange on either side of the membranes to remove each of the segments.

Whisk the olive oil, vinegar, and black pepper together, then stir in the orange segments, capers, and olives.

Drizzle the orange dressing over the cod slices and arrange the onion on top. Scatter the remaining marjoram leaves over the dish and serve.

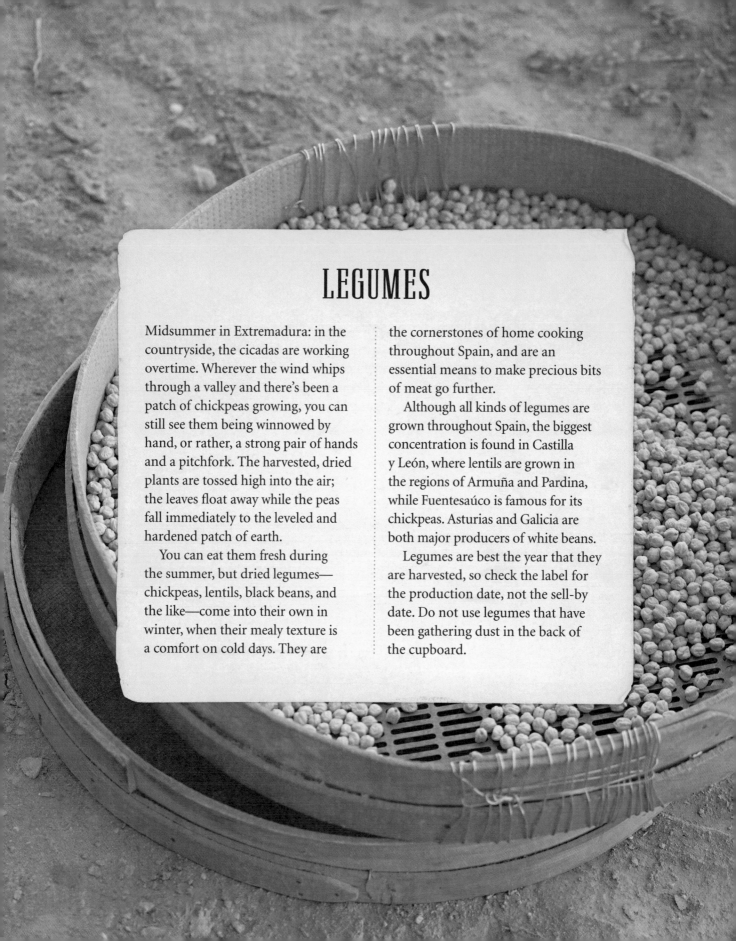

LEGUMES

Midsummer in Extremadura: in the countryside, the cicadas are working overtime. Wherever the wind whips through a valley and there's been a patch of chickpeas growing, you can still see them being winnowed by hand, or rather, a strong pair of hands and a pitchfork. The harvested, dried plants are tossed high into the air; the leaves float away while the peas fall immediately to the leveled and hardened patch of earth.

You can eat them fresh during the summer, but dried legumes—chickpeas, lentils, black beans, and the like—come into their own in winter, when their mealy texture is a comfort on cold days. They are the cornerstones of home cooking throughout Spain, and are an essential means to make precious bits of meat go further.

Although all kinds of legumes are grown throughout Spain, the biggest concentration is found in Castilla y León, where lentils are grown in the regions of Armuña and Pardina, while Fuentesaúco is famous for its chickpeas. Asturias and Galicia are both major producers of white beans.

Legumes are best the year that they are harvested, so check the label for the production date, not the sell-by date. Do not use legumes that have been gathering dust in the back of the cupboard.

LENTIL SALAD WITH PIQUILLO PEPPERS AND ANCHOVIES

This is great as a first course, or as part of a selection of salads. It would go well with a beet salad, for example. I created this dish out of leftovers from a previous day's party and ate it with a plain omelet—it was heaven. If you can't find cans or jars of piquillo peppers, use roasted red peppers instead.

Serves 4

11oz dried green lentils, cooked

6 piquillo peppers, sliced into thin strips

½ red onion, sliced

2 tablespoons salted capers, rinsed

4 tablespoons extra virgin olive oil

2 tablespoons Cabernet red wine vinegar

salt and freshly ground black pepper

handful of mixed herbs, such as mint, chervil, and flat-leaf parsley leaves

16 anchovy fillets in oil

Mix the cooked lentils, peppers, onion, and capers in a bowl. Make a dressing with the oil and vinegar and pour it over the lentil mixture. Season cautiously with salt and pepper, bearing in mind that the anchovies and capers are salty.

Mix in the fresh herbs, divide the salad between four plates, and decorate with the anchovies.

EL TRI...

LEGUMBRES
SELECTAS
Peso Neto: 1 Kg.

LEGUMBRES
SELECTAS
Peso Neto: 1 Kg.

LEGUMBRES
SELECTAS
1 Kg.

LEGUMBRES
SELECTAS
Peso Neto: 1 Kg.

PAN-FRIED HALIBUT WITH BLACK BEANS AND WATERCRESS SALAD

Halibut is a delicious fish: firm-fleshed with a beautiful flavor that goes really well with the beans. Do try and use dried black beans for this recipe—they make a great sauce.

Serves 4

7oz dried black beans
1 small onion, whole
1 small leek, whole
1 tomato, whole
1 small carrot, whole
1 small bay leaf
½ teaspoon spanish smoked paprika (mild)
2 garlic cloves, 1 chopped
3 tablespoons extra virgin olive oil
salt and freshly ground black pepper
4 halibut steaks, 7oz each

watercress salad

large bunch of watercress
2 tablespoons extra virgin olive oil
1 tablespoon Moscatel white wine vinegar
salt and freshly ground black pepper

Soak the beans for 12 hours in plenty of cold water.

In a saucepan, mix the beans with all the vegetables, the bay leaf, paprika, and one of the garlic cloves (whole) in enough fresh water to fill the pan two fingers-width above the beans. Bring everything rapidly to a boil, then reduce the heat to a gentle simmer for about 1 hour. After that time, remove and reserve the vegetables and the garlic clove, and leave the beans in the pan to continue cooking.

In a frying pan, heat 2 tablespoons of olive oil over medium heat and cook the second chopped garlic clove until golden. Now add the cooked garlic, onion, leek, and carrot and season with salt and pepper. Scrape everything into a food processor and process to a purée. You want to thicken the bean liquor with this purée, so once the beans are cooked, carefully mix it in so that the beans do not break.

Wash the watercress thoroughly. To make the dressing, simply whisk the oil, vinegar, and salt and pepper together and toss it through the watercress.

Season the fish with salt before you start cooking them; it tastes better this way. Heat the remaining oil in a non-stick frying pan over medium heat and cook the fillets for about 4 minutes on each side, depending on the thickness of each fillet.

Place a spoonful of beans in the middle of the plate, the fillet of fish on top, and the watercress salad to one side. Drizzle the fish and beans with a little olive oil and serve.

LIMA BEANS WITH CUTTLEFISH

I love this bean and seafood combination, which I made up one evening for my supper. Cuttlefish are called *chocos* in Andalucía; in fact, the inhabitants of Huelva (close to the Portuguese border) eat such large amounts of this cephalopod that they are actually known as *los chocos*.

The most common way to cook cuttlefish is to cut them up into ½in squares, dunk them in flour, and then deep-fry them. Serve with a splash of lemon. If you can't find cuttlefish, you can always use squid.

Serves 4

10oz dried lima beans
5 tablespoons extra virgin
  olive oil
1 small leek, chopped
1 carrot, chopped
1 bay leaf
1 medium onion, chopped
2 small garlic cloves, sliced
2 tomatoes, chopped
salt and freshly ground
  black pepper
1 teaspoon spanish smoked
  paprika (hot)
6 tablespoons dry white wine
1¼lb cuttlefish or squid,
  cleaned and cut into
  small pieces
5 flat-leaf parsley sprigs,
  chopped

Soak the beans for 12 hours in plenty of cold water.

Put the beans in enough fresh water to fill the pan two fingers-width above the beans. Add 2 tablespoons of the olive oil, leek, carrot, and bay leaf, and let cook for between 1 and 2 hours, simmering over low heat. After 30 minutes, add half a glass of cold water, which will improve the final texture of the beans once cooked. When the beans are done, remove the leek and carrot.

In another saucepan, heat 2 tablespoons of olive oil over medium heat and sauté the onion and garlic until soft, which will take about 5 minutes. Add the tomatoes, season with salt and pepper, and cook for 5 minutes before adding the paprika. Stir for 15 seconds, then add the wine, and let the mixture reduce a little before adding the beans and the bean liquor. Simmer for another 5 minutes to let the flavors develop.

Heat a heavy frying pan and season the cuttlefish with salt and pepper. Add 1 tablespoon of oil and, when it is shimmering, fry the cuttlefish very quickly—no more than a minute.

Stir the cuttlefish through the beans, scatter the parsely over the top, and eat immediately.

NAVY BEAN SOUP WITH CLAMS

Legumes and shellfish make a heavenly combination: chickpeas and mussels, borlotti beans and shrimp, I could go on—but this recipe is one of my favorites.

Serves 4

5oz dried navy beans
1 bay leaf
1 thyme sprig
3 tablespoons extra virgin
    olive oil
1 garlic clove, chopped
1 onion, finely chopped
7 saffron threads
6 tablespoons dry sherry
    or white wine
1¼lb clams
2½ cups fish stock
salt and freshly ground
    black pepper
5 flat-leaf parsley sprigs,
    chopped

Soak the beans for 12 hours in plenty of cold water.

Cover the beans in enough fresh water to fill the pan two fingers-width above the beans, add the bay leaf and thyme, and bring to a boil. Once bubbling, reduce the heat and let the beans simmer gently for about 1 hour. Then let cool in the saucepan in their liquid.

While the beans are cooling, heat the oil over medium heat and cook the garlic and onion until golden—about 5 minutes. Add the sherry or wine, then let it bubble for 2 minutes to let the alcohol evaporate. Add the saffron and stir.

Drain the beans and add them to the clams and the fish stock. Season with salt and pepper, then cover with a lid and bring to a boil. Leave for 2 minutes before checking the clams; as soon as they open, take the pan off the heat. Discard any shells that haven't opened. Add a drizzle of olive oil and a sprinkling of flat-leaf parsley and serve.

CHORIZO

The original chorizo was probably invented in Extremadura, which isn't so surprising given that the monks in the region were the first to cultivate the peppers brought back from Mexico. Up to the point where some enterprising cook invented smoked paprika and added it to sausages, the only way to cure meat was with salt.

Chorizo as we know it today is a pork sausage that has been spiced and marinated, then cured for varying lengths of time. The key ingredient is paprika. The *picante* (hot) and *agridulce* (bittersweet and medium-hot) versions tend to be used, though there are myriad variations on the basic recipe, changing from region to region.

In Extremadura, our chorizos taste smoky thanks to the use of smoked paprika (see page 128). In Murcia, on the other hand, the paprika is made from sun-dried rather than smoke-dried peppers, so their chorizos taste quite different. Chorizo is graded according to the meat, fat, and humidity content, with "extra" being the best quality. A ratio of 60 percent lean to 30 percent fat is ideal for chorizo.

Try to buy your chorizo from a deli that has a selection of artisanal chorizos, made using animal intestines for the casings—you can pick them out quite easily because they are a bit lumpy and irregular looking. Natural casings allow the meat to breathe and cure for longer, and the result has a lovely copper color. Chorizos that have a sharp bright color and uniform shape will be cheaper but less tasty, as they will have been fast-cured in industrial drying rooms.

Chorizo never fails to appear on my menus: it is what customers expect to see in a Spanish restaurant. I use the fresh chorizo the most; this is the size and shape of a US sausage and has been cured for only a few days. Hoop-shaped chorizos have been cured for around a month; these can be used for both cooking and eating. Longer-cured chorizos tend to be firmer and more like a salami in texture. Use the latter chopped up as a seasoning, or served sliced as part of a platter of meats.

PAN-FRIED CHORIZO IN CIDER

This is a very popular tapas dish at our restaurant, but at home with my family it's more of a snack.

Serves 4
1 tablespoon extra virgin olive oil
1lb fresh chorizo, cut into
⅜in slices
1 red onion, coarsely chopped
1 garlic clove
1 thyme sprig, leaves stripped
¾ cup dry cider
¾ cup chicken stock

Heat the oil in a frying pan over medium heat and pan-fry the chorizo for 8 minutes. Spoon off any excess fat. Add the onion, garlic, and thyme and sauté for 5 minutes. Next pour in the cider and simmer for 5 minutes before adding the chicken stock. Reduce the heat and gently simmer the mixture for 10 minutes. Season with salt and pepper and serve with hunks of crusty fresh bread to mop up the juices.

CHICKPEAS WITH CHORIZO

This traditional dish is a cross between a soup and a stew and is served in homes all over Spain: that tells you how good it is. It is a great hangover cure, the only problem being that you have to plan your hangover by letting the legumes soak the night before—otherwise you'll have to make do with canned chickpeas. The other problem is that this dish goes really well with a nice bottle of Spanish red wine—so I recommend avoiding that hangover in the first place!

It used to be very important to check for pits if you were using dried chickpeas. My family used to grow chickpeas, so I speak from experience; it's amazing how grit can be the shape of a chickpea, but now this won't be a problem. For a variation, stir in a big handful of fresh spinach at the end.

Serves 4

10oz dried chickpeas
4 tablespoons extra virgin
   olive oil
2 garlic cloves, chopped
1 onion, chopped
2 carrots, chopped
10oz fresh spicy chorizo,
   sliced
9oz dry-cured bacon, cubed
1 quart chicken stock
1 bay leaf
salt and freshly ground
   black pepper
handful of chopped flat-leaf
   parsley (optional)

Soak the chickpeas in lots of cold water for a minimum of 6 hours before you intend to cook them. Overnight is best.

Heat the oil in a saucepan and lightly cook the chopped garlic, onion, and carrots. When the vegetables are nicely golden, add the chorizo and bacon and sauté until the bits are brown all over.

Add the stock and the bay leaf. Bring to a boil, add the chickpeas, and cook for about 1 hour—nibble on one occasionally to check if it's cooked. While they are cooking, skim off any foam or chorizo fat that comes to the surface.

Once the chickpeas are soft but not mushy, season to taste with salt and pepper Add a little boiling water if you like a more soupy consistency.

Divide the soup between four bowls, drizzle a little olive oil over the top, and scatter over some parsley if you have any. And don't forget that bottle of red wine!

LA MATANZA

As a child in a small village of less than one thousand people, this was the most thrilling thing to experience. The *matanza* (literally "pig slaughter") was the biggest party of the year, with everyone joining in, eating and drinking and working hard. It was particularly exciting for me because my family's *matanza* was just before Christmas.

I used to wake up at six in the morning, or earlier, when it was all cold and crisp and the sun hadn't yet crept over the horizon, and ride down to the farmyard. The only other person stirring was the baker, surrounding himself in warm wafts of vanilla. I'd be hugging the pig before anyone else arrived, totally unfazed at the prospect of the pig's fate, even though it had been my friend for the year.

That pig was mine! I'd hang onto the tail while the strongest man in the village took the squealing pig from the sty. The tail was the bit that I—as the youngest in the group—was going to eat, the trophy to chew in triumph.

The pig had to be put onto a table with its head hanging over the edge, so that the blood could be drained into a bucket after its throat had been cut. The scariest thing was not the pig's screams but the slaughterman and his huge sharp knife, which in one quick movement he'd thrust into the animal's jugular and slit the throat. And the blood: there was literally steaming quarts of the stuff and absolutely none of it would be wasted.

The mother of my best girlfriend had the job of stirring the blood with her hands—she'd be in it up to her elbows—to keep it from coagulating. Every so often, she'd scoop out the sticky proteins, and throw the gloop to an expectant cat.

After the animal had been bled, the next step was to singe the hair off; the smell is unpleasant to say the least. We didn't use gas blowtorches in those days, but a fiercely spiny broom plant that we'd gather a month or so before the big day. Murderous clumps of this shrub would be hung to dry in the outbuildings, ready to be set alight on the big day. A fire is essential at a *matanza*, both to remove the bristles from the pig's carcass, but also to keep the cold at bay.

Tasks were divided along gender lines. For the men, it was the butchering of the carcass. For the women, it was dealing with the offal and cleaning the intestines: not a pleasant job, but nevertheless essential as the guts are used as sausage casings—and there's a sausage in Spain for every part of the intestine.

To make sure that the animal was fit to eat, two pieces of meat had to be dispatched to the vet. We'd have to wait about 30 minutes for the results to come back, during which time everyone nibbled on bread and jam. Only once the pig was declared disease-free could we have a breakfast of grilled pork. Not for me, however: the first thing I ate was that prized tail.

Everyone spends the day eating. The liver and brains were pan-fried on the day in a coating of flour and egg. Traditionally, the last dish to be eaten was *la prueba* ("the test"). When you make chorizo, you have to test the meat filling to see how it's going to turn out: is there enough paprika, too much salt, and so on. So the meat is fried and eaten with a big bowl of salad (my dad can pull lettuce from November onward).

At the end of the day, the hams would be curing in salt, the sausages hanging in a cool place, and I would go to bed totally exhausted but happy.

As an adult, I look back on the *matanza* with mixed emotions. Let's face it, it's not the best way to kill a pig, and most children in the US would be terrified. But it was a fact of life in rural Spain, and you learned at a very early age exactly where your meat came from. Nowadays, the traditional *matanza* has gone; thanks to health and safety regulations, the pig has to be killed in an abattoir. But the memory and spirit of the occasion live on in the hearts of most country-living Spaniards.

MORCILLA

Morcilla is known in the US as blood sausage; the French call it *boudin noir* and the British call it black pudding. It's a typical product of the *matanza*, a way to use up all the blood.

There are different types and numerous different recipes for each type, so you come across morcilla flavored with anything from cloves to cumin; the famous Guadalupe monastery kitchens add *pimentón de la Vera picante* (hot smoked paprika). *Morcilla de Burgos*, which contains rice, is the most widespread in Spain, but my favorite is the one that I grew up with, *morcilla de cebolla*, which contains onion and is produced in Extremadura and Catalonia. Part of the reason I particularly like it is because you can boil, grill, fry, or even stew it.

It sounds obvious, but the only way to ensure that you are buying a good morcilla is to track down a really good Spanish deli or butcher. And have a good look at the sausage: it should have a slightly crumbly texture and not too much fat. The color before you cook it is dark brown, and the sausage only goes black once it's cooked (usually grilled or pan-fried).

Morcilla goes well with eggs, apples, peppers, beans, and tomato sauce. The sausage has a very short shelf life and so, traditionally, it's a winter thing. Traditionally, the best time to eat one is three or four days after the *matanza*.

SCRAMBLED EGGS WITH MORCILLA

This dish is quite rich, so you will probably want to go for a healthy walk afterward! The combination of the creamy scrambled eggs and the strong, velvety morcilla definitely needs something else to balance it, hence the mint, which provides a palate-cleansing zing to the dish.

Serves 4

1 tablespoon extra virgin
   olive oil
7oz morcilla or blood
   sausage, skin removed
1 garlic clove, finely chopped
8 large free-range eggs
salt and ground black pepper
4 mint sprigs, leaves
   stripped and chopped
handful of pine nuts, toasted

Heat the olive oil in a pan. Break up the sausage into chunks and cook over high heat with the garlic for a minute or two.

I don't beat the eggs before I add them to the pan; I just drop them in and start beating; this breaks up the sausage even more, but that's OK. The eggs should be set and creamy but not solid. Season to taste with salt and pepper, but be careful as the morcilla has a very strong flavor.

Stir through the mint, sprinkle the pine nuts over the top, and serve immediately.

SAUTÉED MORCILLA WITH MINT OIL

This is a fabulous brunch or appetizer. If you cannot find cans or jars of piquillo peppers, use jarred roasted red peppers instead. The mint oil keeps well in the fridge and is great with lots of other dishes, such as grilled lamb or pan-fried fish.

Serves 4

mint oil
small bunch of mint
6 tablespoons extra virgin
  olive oil
salt and freshly ground
  black pepper

morcilla
2 dessert apples, preferably
  McIntosh or russet
1 tablespoon extra virgin
  olive oil
14oz morcilla or blood
  sausage
4oz piquillo peppers, drained
  and cut into strips
¼ cup toasted almond slivers
2 slices of bread, toasted and
  cut in half

First, make the mint oil. Strip the leaves from the stalks and blanch in boiling water for 20 seconds. Drain and refresh in iced water, then squeeze out the excess moisture until you have a walnut-sized lump of leaves. Loosen them out and let cool. When the mint has cooled, add the oil, salt, and pepper and blend using a hand blender or a food processor.

Now core, peel, and chop the apple into cubes. Heat the oil in a frying pan over medium heat until it shimmers, then add the apple pieces and cook them until they start to turn brown and sticky around the edges.

Remove the casing from the the sausage and, using your hands, break up the mixture into chunks. Add to the frying pan and mix it up with the apple. Stir regularly to keep everything from sticking too much, and sauté until the morcilla is black in color. This will take about 5 minutes. Spoon off any excess fat that appears.

Morcilla needs a bit of help to look attractive. So, place a 4in cookie cutter on a warmed plate and spoon in a quarter of the mixture. Lay the pepper strips across the top, scatter with a few almonds, then carefully lift off the cutter. Lean a toast triangle against the sausage and finish off with a drizzle of mint oil. Repeat three more times.

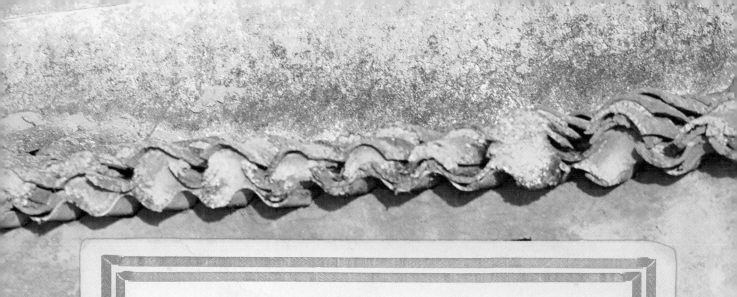

OFFAL

Offal is a regular item on the family menu—after all, nothing is wasted—but it wasn't until I worked in Madrid that I really started to appreciate how these animal bits and pieces can be gourmet food. Many people in the US and UK are notoriously cautious about offal, but my customers have become more and more adventurous, so these days I always make sure that there is some offal on the menu at my restaurant.

Offal is not only good for you, it's also really good value for your money. The main thing to remember is to choose offal from a young animal, and to buy it from a trusted butcher.

SAUTÉED CHICKEN LIVERS WITH CAPERS

My mother likes to cook liver until it is really well done. I love her, of course, but I think my way of cooking liver is better! The trick is to cook them until medium rare.

Fresh livers have a nice shine and are a purple-brown color. Avoid livers that have a limp brown look to them. To prepare livers, simply remove the yellow veins from the lobes and that's it!

Serves 4

3 tablespoons extra virgin olive oil
1 large shallot, finely chopped
2 garlic cloves, finely chopped
14oz free-range chicken livers
salt and freshly ground black pepper
2 tablespoons sherry vinegar
2 tablespoons salted capers, rinsed
5 flat-leaf parsley sprigs, chopped
4 slices of good-quality bread
1 small red onion, finely sliced
4 mint spigs, leaves chopped

Heat the olive oil in a frying pan and sauté the shallot and garlic until soft but not colored. Add the livers, season with salt and pepper, and cook for about 4 minutes. Pour in the vinegar and reduce for 3 minutes more, by which time the vinegar smell should have disappeared. Stir in the capers and parsley.

Toast the bread and cut each slice in half, making two triangles. Arrange on a plate and top with the livers, followed by a scattering of red onion and chopped mint, and serve.

LAMB'S KIDNEYS COOKED IN SHERRY

This dish is typical of Andalucía. It makes an excellent supper dish, served with olive oil-flavored mashed potatoes (see page 130).

Lamb's kidneys need to be thoroughly cleaned, so I recommend doing the following whenever you use them. First, quarter the kidneys, then let them soak for 15 minutes in acidulated, salted water: for every 2 cups water you will need ¼ cup vinegar and 1 teaspoon of salt. Rinse them in clean water. Heat a tablespoon of olive oil in a wok and stir-fry the kidneys for 4 minutes. Discard the juices, rinse in water, then pat dry. The kidneys are now ready for use.

Serves 4

4 tablespoons extra virgin olive oil
1 small white onion, thinly sliced
3 garlic cloves, sliced
10 lamb's kidneys, prepared as above
salt and freshly ground black pepper
½ cup dry sherry, preferably Fino
mashed potatoes, to serve (see page 130)
¼ cup pine nuts, toasted
5 flat-leaf parsley sprigs, chopped (optional)
extra virgin olive oil, for drizzling

Heat the oil in a frying pan over medium heat. Add the onion and garlic and sauté until soft, about 3 minutes, then stir in the kidneys. Season with salt and pepper, add the sherry, and let everything simmer for 5 minutes or until reduced to a creamy consistency.

Place a large dollop of mashed potatoes on four warmed plates, followed by some of the kidney mixture. Drizzle a small teaspoon of your most special extra virgin olive oil over everything, then scatter the pine nuts over the top, and some chopped parsley, if you want to add some extra color.

PAN-FRIED FOIE GRAS WITH BRAISED LENTILS

This dish always sells out whenever it's on the menu. We source our livers from suppliers in London's Borough Market, who make sure that they come from trusted producers. The way to judge a good foie gras isn't difficult: the liver should look shiny, pale, and firm without too many veins, and it should not smell at all. It will be too late if you discover this, but good liver shouldn't melt once it is cooked.

If you can buy Pardina lentils, which are grown near Salamanca, that's great. If not, Puy lentils are a good substitute.

Serves 4

braised lentils
1 tablespoon extra virgin
   olive oil
1 shallot, finely chopped
1 carrot, finely chopped
1 bay leaf
5oz dried small green lentils
2 cups chicken stock, cold
salt and freshly ground
   black pepper

6 tablespoons sherry vinegar
4 scallops of foie gras (each
   approx. 4oz)
5 flat-leaf parsley sprigs
   chopped

To make the braised lentils, heat the oil in a saucepan and cook the shallot, carrot, and bay leaf until they begin to turn golden. Add the lentils and the cold chicken stock, give everything a good stir, and let cook for 20 to 25 minutes. Season with salt and pepper at the end of cooking.

Put the sherry vinegar into a small saucepan over low heat and let it reduce until there is about a quarter of the vinegar left. (I think a slow reduction is better than a rapid boil—it's less likely to burn and the flavors have a chance to mellow.)

When the lentils are cooked, heat a non-stick frying pan over high heat, then carefully slide in the foie gras. Brown for about 1 minute on each side, then remove and lay on paper towels to drain. Season with salt and pepper.

Divide the lentils and a little of their juices between four soup bowls. Top with the foie gras, then drizzle over the sherry vinegar sauce followed by the parsley and serve.

SPANISH HAM

The Spanish have a rather complicated relationship with pigs. Some folks—me included—treat them as pets, but then happily kill them; others hold the animals in disdain and hide them away, but revere the meat. One thing is for sure though: Spain produces the best air-dried ham in the world.

In ham-producing regions there are butchers who sell *jamón* and nothing else. They provide a good opportunity for you to judge for yourself how the flavor of the ham varies according to both the breed of pig and the pigs' diet.

There are two main types of Spanish ham: *jamón Ibérico*, made from the black-hoofed Ibérico pig, a descendant of the Mediterranean wild boar; and *jamón Serrano*, produced from a modern breed of white pig. Although the latter can in

principle be made wherever there are white pigs to be found, *serrano* means "from the mountains," and the best hams still come from Spain's mountainous regions. My favorite Serrano ham comes from Teruel in Aragón, and has *Denominación de Origen* status.

Ibérico ham is special because there are only two regions in Spain where Ibérico pigs are reared. Extremadura is one of them. My pig farmer friends, the Roa brothers, are passionate about their business. The pigs are reared and the hams cured on their farm, and they are involved in the whole process from piglet to plate. The brothers love their ham so much that I suspect they eat it for breakfast, lunch, and dinner every day of the year.

It's a great sight to see their pigs trotting daintily through the *dehesa* (wooded pastures) in November and December, foraging for acorns, their traditional diet. Sadly, there are no longer enough acorns to feed all the Ibérico pigs reared in Spain, so Ibérico ham is graded according to the amount of acorns in their diet.

If a pig has grazed solely on acorns and grass for the last six months of its life, then the resulting ham is called *jamón Ibérico de bellota* (acorn-fed Iberian ham), which is the most expensive version. Whichever type of Ibérico ham you buy, make sure you eat it freshly carved at room temperature—and please enjoy the fat. Ibérico pigs are unique in their ability to transform more than half of their fat into "good fat" with properties similar to olive oil.

Both Serrano and Ibérico hams are primarily eaten as a snack. The slices are not served long and thin, but instead are carved by hand into roughly 2in pieces called *virutas*, or shavings. Serrano ham is also used a lot in cooking: it has a wonderful affinity with seafood, but you will find small quantities in everything from bean stews to salads. In cooking, Serrano ham is often used diced rather than in thin slices, so try to find a deli that can cut the ham to order.

HAM CROQUETAS

Croquetas are one of the most popular dishes in my tapas restaurant. I spent ages perfecting this recipe. Usually the roux is made with butter, but I use olive oil because I think it gives a better flavor. In Spanish delis you can often buy cubed Ibérico ham (left over from carving the legs), which is ideal for this recipe—meat from close to the bone has the best flavor. If you cannot get ahold of Ibérico ham, use Serrano ham instead, or indeed other cured hams such as prosciutto. *Croquetas* are a bit of a hassle to make, but they can be frozen and make great party food, so give them a try.

Makes 15 to 20 croquetas

4 tablespoons extra virgin olive oil

½ small leek, diced as small as possible (⅛ in pieces)

3oz Ibérico or other air-dried ham, diced very small

½ cup flour

⅓ cup ham or vegetable stock

1¼ cups whole milk

freshly grated nutmeg

salt and freshly ground black pepper

⅔ cup flour

2 large free-range eggs, beaten

⅔ cup dried breadcrumbs

olive oil, for frying

Heat the olive oil in a pan until it starts to shimmer, then add the leek and sauté until soft but not colored. Stir in the ham, cook for another minute, then stir in the ½ cup flour and cook over medium heat until the mixture is golden but not burnt. This will take about 5 minutes. It is important that the flour is cooked properly otherwise the *croquetas* will taste like flour.

Combine the stock and milk in a pan and heat until hot but not boiling. Season the liquid with a few scrapes of nutmeg. Gradually add the liquid to the roux, a few tablespoons at a time, stirring the mixture all the time. Once you have incorporated all the milk, continue to cook the sauce for about 10 minutes until it thickens and leaves the sides of the pan when you stir it. At this stage, add a couple of twists of the pepper mill, taste the roux, and adjust the salt if necessary—the ham can be very salty to start with. The sauce is now done: it's got to be really thick because you don't want the *croquetas* to turn into pancakes! Smooth the sauce on to a baking sheet (8in x 12in is fine) then cover with plastic wrap to keep the mixture from drying out. Let cool before putting it in the fridge for an hour.

When you are ready for the next stage, line up three bowls: one with flour, the other with beaten egg, and the third with the breadcrumbs. Take the sauce out of the fridge.

Dust your hands with flour, make a ball with the ham mixture, and roll it between your palms. The size and shape of the croquetas is up to you, but the easiest is a walnut-sized ball. Next, dunk the croqueta into the flour—you want a dusting—followed by the egg and then the breadcrumbs. Put the croquetas on a tray and when you've used up all the mixture, put them all back in the fridge for 30 minutes.

If you have a deep-fryer, heat the oil to 325°F and fry the croquetas for a couple of minutes. If not, heat the oil in a frying pan until it starts to shimmer, then add 3 or 4 croquetas at a time and fry until they are golden all over.

PORK FILLET WITH PIQUILLO PEPPERS

I use fillets from Ibérico pigs for this recipe when I offer it on my tapas menu: the flesh is dark, flavorsome, and meltingly tender, thanks to the diet of acorns that the pigs enjoy in the autumn and winter. When animals have been raised under such carefully monitored conditions, it is OK to serve the meat rare—which is what this recipe calls for—and it is as succulent as rare beef fillet.

Having said that, it is very difficult to source fresh Ibérico pork outside the restaurant industry, so I recommend tracking down the best free-range pork available in your area, a rare breed variety perhaps, and increasing the cooking time a little so you end up with a medium-cooked fillet. This dish is wonderful with olive oil mashed potatoes (see page 130) and a green salad.

Serves 4

4 pork fillets, approx. 9oz each
3 tablespoons extra virgin
  olive oil
1 teaspoon spanish smoked
  paprika (bittersweet)
2 oregano sprigs, leaves
  stripped and chopped
1 garlic clove, finely chopped
½ teaspoon ground cumin
salt and freshly ground
  black pepper
8 piquillo peppers

Mix the pork with all the other ingredients except for the peppers and let marinate in the fridge for a minimum of 12 hours.

Bring the meat to room temperature while you preheat the oven to 425°F.

Place the pork fillets on a baking sheet and roast until the meat has reached the desired doneness (8 minutes for rare meat). Add another 3 minutes of cooking time for ordinary pork fillets. Let the meat rest for 5 minutes.

Lay two peppers across each fillet on each plate, drizzle with a little olive oil, and serve immediately.

PORK PRESERVED IN OLIVE OIL

This dish, known as *lomo de orza* in Spain, is so good! The *orza* in the name refers to the earthenware dish in which the pork is marinated. This method of cooking pork apparently comes from the Jaén province of Andalucía, but I first ate it in a Madrid tapas bar, served on thick chewy toast. You can also serve this dish with a bitter frisée salad, as it will balance the richness of the pork.

Serves 6

marinade

4 garlic cloves, finely sliced
  lengthwise
3 oregano sprigs, leaves
  stripped
1 rosemary sprig
1 thyme sprig
½ cup sherry vinegar
½ cup dry white wine
1 tablespoon peppercorns

1¾lb boneless pork loin, cut
  into 1¼in-thick steaks
sea salt
¾ cup extra virgin olive oil
1 lemon

Mix the marinade ingredients in a glass bowl. Add the pork, cover, and let sit in the fridge for 24 hours.

The next day, remove the pork from the marinade and pat dry. Set the marinade to one side. Season the pork with salt.

Heat half the olive oil in a large frying pan over medium to high heat and cook the pork slices for 4 minutes on each side so that the pork is cooked, but still juicy.

Put the meat and the cooking juices back into the marinade and add the rest of the oil, making sure that you cover the meat completely. The pork will now keep for a couple of weeks in the fridge, or you can eat it immediately.

Make sure that you take the pork out of the fridge a good 30 minutes before you want to eat it. Cut the meat on the diagonal into very thin strips, and arrange on a large plate. Spoon over the oily marinade followed by a squeeze of lemon juice.

PIG'S EARS

We have a saying in Spain: "*Del cerdo, se come hasta los andares,*" which basically means that we eat every last bit of a pig, down to its trotters. And pig's ears are a great delicacy—I adore them! So much so that my mother always makes this snack for me when I go home.

Pig's ears have a delicate taste, and a texture rather like a granular shiitake mushroom: a bit gelatinous or slippery and a bit crunchy.

Some butchers don't like to sell pig's ears—they get more money for them if they are ground up for sausage meat. So they may need a bit of persuasion to sell you two whole ones for this dish.

Serves 4
2 pig's ears
1 onion, sliced
1 leek, cut into chunky slices
2 carrots, coarsely chopped
2 bay leaves
sea salt and black
   peppercorns

sofrito
1 tablespoon extra virgin
   olive oil
1 onion, finely diced
2 garlic cloves, finely diced
6 tablespoons white wine
1 teaspoon spanish smoked
   paprika (hot)

First, cook the pig's ears. Simply put everything in a saucepan and cover with water. Boil for 2 hours, topping off with water if necessary and removing any foam that comes to the surface. Keep simmering until you can stick a knife into the thickest part of the ear very easily. Let the ears cool, then use a pair of scissors to cut them up into ¾in squares.

For the sofrito, heat the oil in a frying pan and sauté the onion until soft but not colored. Make a paste with the garlic cloves and the wine in a pestle and mortar. Stir this into the onions along with the paprika, then add the chopped-up pig's ears. Simmer until the wine has evaporated and you are left with an oniony coating on the pork.

Eat as a snack or a tapas dish.

PORK CHOPS WITH GARLIC AND CHILE DRESSING

The garlic and chile dressing in this recipe comes from the Basque Country, where cooks like to serve it with the head of a hake, which has delicious succulent morsels of sweet flesh to be picked out. I adapted it to go with pork chops one day when I was cooking the restaurant staff lunch and wanted to spice the dish up a bit, but had very little time. It makes an ideal midweek supper dish.

Serves 4

- 4 pork loin chops (approx. 9oz each)
- 1 red chile pepper
- 2 garlic cloves
- 4 tablespoons extra virgin olive oil
- 2 tablespoons sherry vinegar
- 1 bag of herb salad, such as a mixture of cilantro, flat-leaf parsley, and arugula

Preheat the broiler. Place the chops on a grill pan under medium heat for around 8 minutes on each side, until the juices run clear and there is no pink meat.

Meanwhile, seed the chile, being sure to wash your hands well afterward. Finely slice the chile followed by the garlic cloves.

A couple of minutes before you think the pork chops are ready, heat the oil in a frying pan and sauté the garlic and chile until the garlic is golden. Add the vinegar—please be very careful as it will spit—and stir once.

Divide the salad between four plates, place a pork chop on one side, and pour the hot dressing over the top. Eat immediately, with chunks of fresh crusty bread.

CHRISTMAS IN SPAIN

For me, Christmas always started with the making of a *nacimiento*, a tableau of the nativity scene, which was usually placed on a table in a prominent place such as our living room or by the entrance into church. My best friend Elsa and I had the self-imposed responsibility to make one for the church, our school, and the old people's home. We were in demand and we loved doing it, not having the distractions in those days of the television or PlayStation.

Elsa and I started work in the second week of December. We would get up really early and collect tough grass from the hillside above our village. This was used to make the ground cover. Of course foliage wasn't the only thing on our minds; we had a lovely time foraging for snacks, such as pine nuts and fruit from the *madroños* or strawberry trees.

Once back home we had to build the set and then dress it, and one way or another it would take us the entire afternoon to complete a scene. Each nativity scene was different, not least because we didn't have enough figures to go around. A bit like families and their Christmas tree decorations in northern Europe, we collected and edited our figures and scenery over the years. Elaborate Virgin Marys, stoic donkeys, and palm trees—I have fond memories of them all, but my favorite was *el hombre cagando* (literally, "the man crapping"), who had to be put somewhere well away from the crib. It is not just me, by the way, he is a popular character you will find in a lot of *nacimientos*!

On Christmas Eve, before dinner, all the village children went carol-singing around the houses for money or sweets. Then we had dinner with Granny Faustina, my father's mother. She loved cooking—in fact, it's all she seemed to do with her days. Her traditional Christmas Eve meal consisted of a first course of clear chicken broth served with a special kind of fried bread, similar to croutons, followed by a partridge stew. We weren't dessert fans, so the meal was rounded off with a selection of *turrón*, or almond sweets from Alicante (similar to nougat). My favorite was the chocolate version.

Having barely digested dinner, I'd rush off to do my duty as choirboy at midnight mass and then collapse in bed, untroubled by thoughts of Santa Claus.

Christmas Day was a very low-key affair: nowadays, children receive some presents, but when I was growing up, the highlight of the day was lunch. Typically, we had a simple platter of steamed seafood to start with, followed by roast lamb—and of course more turrón. More recently, thanks to the Costa Tropical near Granada, pineapples are now available and we like to have it at the end of the meal.

Children had to wait for the three kings to arrive on Twelfth Night for their presents. Actually, the present-receiving ritual started on the day before, when there was a procession of three "kings" on horseback around the village to the church. They'd tie up the horses (the bronze tethering rings have been there for centuries) and take up their positions in front of the altar for a service. Only then could the kids approach their favorite king with a letter—or, to be more exact, a wish list of presents. My favorite was Baltasar, the black king (or rather the blacked-up king, as after kissing him I'd be covered in make-up).

The next day, I'd wake up to a present next to our *nacimiento*. I was really upset the year that I discovered my present in the cupboard of my parents' bedroom. I'd been tipped off that the kings didn't really deliver your dreams.

PARTRIDGE STEW

You will occasionally find game butchers in Spain, but most people come by their partridge thanks to friends or by hunting it themselves. In Spain, there is a TV channel devoted to hunting—it is that popular! When you see a bunch of guys in the middle of nowhere with guns, laughing and joking, and taking swigs of something fiery from their hip flasks, it may seem that a day's shooting is simply a brilliant tactic to get out of the house and avoid all those domestic chores. Not so. Flavorwise, wild game is rated very highly, and the farmed equivalents are merely pale imitations.

This is the stew that my family eats on Christmas Eve. The best partridge are from around Toledo—and, of course, Extremadura—but you can use any type of partridge available in your area. Alternatively, you could use quail. This stew tastes wonderful just with a crunchy green salad.

Serves 4

4 partridge
salt and freshly ground
  black pepper
4 tablespoons extra virgin
  olive oil
4 garlic cloves, sliced
3 medium onions, sliced
2 medium carrots, sliced
1 red bell pepper, sliced
2 bay leaves
1 teaspoon black peppercorns
pinch of sea salt
4 thyme sprigs
1 bottle dry white wine
2 tablespoons sherry vinegar
5 flat-leaf parsley sprigs,
  chopped

Pat the partridge dry, inside and out, with paper towels. Tie string around the legs and the wings to keep the birds looking neat. Season with salt and pepper.

Heat the olive oil over medium heat in a large, heavy-based, cast-iron casserole pot and brown the birds on all sides. Remove from the pan and spoon out half of the oil.

With the pan still on the heat, add the garlic and onions and stir for several minutes—you'll find that the onions will pick up the delicious caramelized residue on the base of the pan. Once this has happened, add the carrots and pepper. Let the vegetables sauté for about 10 minutes until they're soft.

Put the partridge back into the casserole, along with the bay leaves, peppercorns, a small pinch of salt, the thyme, white wine, and vinegar. Bring to a boil and remove any foam that comes to the surface.

Cover and let the casserole simmer for anything between 40 and 60 minutes—it depends on whether you are using farmed or wild birds. The latter will take longer to cook. (If you are using quail, simmer for 20 minutes.)

Remove the string from the birds, joint them if you wish, then return them to their juices and stir in the parsley.

RABBIT STEW WITH CELERIAC PURÉE

Like most country folk in Spain, we keep rabbits for eating: there's a large run next to the farmyard and this gives us a steady supply of meat throughout the year. My brother also shoots wild rabbits during the hunting season. Wild rabbit has a gamey flavor and takes longer to cook; the cooking time given in this recipe is for a domestically reared rabbit. When it comes to jointing the rabbit, it's easier to get your butcher to do it for you. Make sure you ask them to leave the front legs whole and the back legs jointed at the knee. This flavorsome stew pairs beautifully with Tempranillo.

Serves 4

marinade

1 bottle red wine
2 rosemary sprigs
2 thyme sprigs
1 head of garlic, halved
1 bay leaf
1 teaspoon black peppercorns
1 rabbit, jointed into 10 pieces

stew

4 tablespoons extra virgin
 olive oil
2 carrots, sliced
1 onion, diced
4 celery ribs, sliced
2oz dried cèps, soaked in
 1 quart hot water
3oz golden raisins (sultanas)
salt and freshly ground
 black pepper

celeriac purée

2 celeriac roots, cleaned
 (approx. 1¾lb)
1 quart milk
2 tablespoons extra virgin
 olive oil

5 flat-leaf parsley sprigs,
 chopped
¼ cup pine nuts, toasted

Put all the marinade ingredients in a large bowl. Add the rabbit, cover, and let marinate in the fridge for at least 12 hours.

When you are ready to cook the stew, remove the meat from the marinade and pat the pieces dry. Reserve the marinade, including the herbs and garlic.

To make the stew, heat the olive oil in a heavy-based casserole or pan. Brown the rabbit pieces and set to one side. Remove the garlic from the marinade and cook in the pan until golden brown, then discard it; you just want garlic-flavored oil.

Cook the carrots, onion, and celery for 5 minutes until the vegetables are softened and golden. Return the rabbit to the pan and add the marinade. Let it bubble for about 8 minutes to reduce a little and to make sure that the alcohol has evaporated. Now add the cèps, along with the liquid in which the mushrooms have been soaking.

Cover the stew and leave to simmer very slowly for an hour, until the rabbit is practically falling off the bone with tenderness. Add the raisins to the stew 15 minutes before the end of cooking. Adjust the seasoning.

Meanwhile, make the celeriac purée. Peel and cut the roots into ¾in pieces. Season the milk with salt and pepper and simmer the celeriac in the milk in a non-stick saucepan. Stir the contents regularly, as you don't want the milk to burn on the base of the pan. Keep cooking until you can poke a knife very easily through the celeriac flesh. This will take about 30 minutes.

Drain the celeriac and mash it with the olive oil. Adjust the seasoning if necessary.

Stir the chopped parsley through the stew and divide between four warmed plates. Place a mound of celeriac purée to one side and ladle over some of the juices. Scatter the toasted pine nuts over the top and serve.

ESCABECHE

The simmered vinegar-and-spice marinade of the escabeche was used traditionally to help preserve a glut of meat or fish for another few days. As a result, Spanish cooks created a whole new dish. An escabeche is a great way to cut the richness of, say, sardines, and can also add interest to potentially bland meat such as farmed rabbit.

QUAIL SALAD ESCABECHE

I have fond memories of watching a quail hen rush through the undergrowth in the *dehesa* (wooded pastures) with a scattering of fifteen chicks trying to keep up with her. It has become an increasingly rare sight, and these days the quail you see in a game butcher's will be farmed. I developed this recipe while in Madrid. The luscious sticky flesh of the dried fruits balances the acidity, while the vinegar stimulates the appetite.

Serves 4

4 quail
salt and ground black pepper
4 tablespoons extra virgin
    olive oil
3 garlic cloves, finely sliced
2 large carrots, diced
2 celery ribs, diced
1 large onion, diced
1 teaspoon black peppercorns
1 bay leaf
2 thyme sprigs
1 rosemary sprig
6 tablespoons dry white wine
6 tablespoons sherry vinegar
1¾ cups chicken stock
8 dried apricots
12 sultanas (golden raisins)
8 prunes, pitted and halved
handful of frisée lettuce
    leaves
2 mint sprigs, leaves
    stripped

First, butterfly the quail by cutting down the backbone and spreading them flat. Trim the wing tips. Pat salt and freshly ground black pepper into the skins.

Heat the oil in a large frying pan over medium heat and cook the birds for 4 to 5 minutes until golden on one side. Turn them over and repeat the process, and then set aside.

Add the garlic to the frying pan and sauté for a minute before adding the carrots, celery, and onion. Sauté the vegetables until they are soft, which will take about 5 minutes.

Add the peppercorns, herbs, wine, and sherry vinegar and bring to a boil. Let the alcohol evaporate—which will take about 4 minutes—and remove any foam that comes to the surface.

Return the birds to the mixture, along with the stock. When it comes to a boil, add the fruit, boil for 30 seconds, and remove from the heat. Let the birds marinate for 3 to 4 hours; in fact, they taste even better the next day.

Mix the frisée and mint leaves and divide between four plates. Season with salt and pepper. Cut the birds in half and arrange them on each plate. Add 3 tablespoons of the escabeche liquid and decorate with the fruit.

ROAST DUCK WITH QUINCE ESCABECHE

We always had a flock of white ducks when I was a child. We kept them for eggs. It wasn't until I moved to Madrid that I ate duck meat for the first time.

I have based the cooking times on a farmed duck with large amounts of breast meat. If you are using wild mallard, you will need two birds for this dish; adjust the cooking time accordingly.

Serves 4

quince escabeche

½ cup soft brown sugar
¾ cup Moscatel or white
   wine vinegar
juice and zest of 1 unwaxed
   orange
2 whole cloves
1 dried red chile pepper
1 star anise
2 cups water
3 large quinces, peeled, cored,
   and quartered

roast duck

1 free-range duck (approx.
   3¼lb)
2 tablespoons extra virgin
   olive oil
salt and freshly ground
   black pepper

salad

¼ cup toasted whole
   hazelnuts, coarsely chopped
2 bunches of watercress,
   thoroughly rinsed
2 mint sprigs, leaves stripped
   and chopped

Put all the escabeche ingredients, except for the quinces, in a saucepan and bring to a boil. Then add the quinces and simmer until the pieces are tender. This can take anywhere from 10 to 20 minutes, depending on the firmness and size of the quince pieces. Decant the fruit and the syrup into a suitable container and let them marinate in the fridge until needed.

Preheat the oven to 425°F.

Lightly season the duck with olive oil, salt, and pepper and roast for 20 minutes. Reduce the oven temperature to 350°F and continue to roast the duck for another 60 minutes. Once cooked, remove the meat from the carcass in hearty chunks, not polite slices.

Bring the quinces to room temperature before serving. Take the quinces and several spoonfuls of the escabeche and mix them with the salad ingredients. Arrange this quince and watercress salad on a large platter, then place the warm duck pieces on top. Let your guests help themselves.

VENISON BURGERS WITH DATE SALSA

Roasting or stewing are the most popular ways to cook venison in Spain, but here is a tasty, more modern recipe.

Makes 4 burgers

burgers
1¼lb ground venison
1 small onion, very finely diced
1 large free-range egg, beaten
1 thyme sprig, leaves removed
salt and freshly ground black pepper
5 flat-leaf parsley sprigs, chopped
3 tablespoons extra virgin olive oil

date and orange salsa
3 oranges, peeled, segments chopped
8 dates, chopped finely
8 small gherkins, diced
2 tablespoons extra virgin olive oil
salt and freshly ground black pepper

to serve
4 buns
romaine lettuce

Mix all the burger ingredients together, except the olive oil, and then make four patties roughly 1in thick. Cover and refrigerate for a few hours.

Bring the burgers to room temperature, then heat the oil in a large frying pan over medium heat. For medium-rare burgers, cook them for 4 to 5 minutes on each side.

While the burgers are cooking, mix the salsa ingredients together in a small bowl.

Split and toast the buns, add a burger to each, and top with a spoonful of salsa and a few romaine lettuce leaves.

CHICKEN PEPITORIA

This is a popular Christmas or celebration dish in Extremadura. *Pepitoria* is a name given to poultry cooked in a mixture of almonds, garlic, and egg. Every family has its own variation—some cooks add nutmeg, others use saffron, although I use neither. You can also use more Christmas-like turkey joints if you prefer. The success of this dish relies on great quality ingredients—so, no cheating with a stock cube! Although fries are the favorite accompaniment to this dish in Spain, it is excellent with boiled potatoes and a simple green salad.

Serves 4
½ cup flour
salt and freshly ground black pepper
3¼lb free-range chicken, jointed into 10 pieces
4 tablespoons extra virgin olive oil
2 bay leaves
6 garlic cloves, crushed
¾ cup dry white wine
approx. 2 cups flavorsome chicken stock
handful of chopped flat-leaf parsley
¼ cup toasted almond slivers
¾ cup whole almonds, toasted and ground
2 large free-range egg yolks

Put the flour in a bowl and season with salt and pepper. Evenly coat the chicken pieces in the flour.

Heat the oil in a cast-iron casserole until it shimmers, then cook the chicken pieces a few at a time until golden brown all over—this will take about 10 minutes. Return all the chicken to the casserole. Add the bay leaves and stir in the garlic purée. Add the wine and enough stock to cover the chicken. Cover and simmer over medium heat for 30 to 35 minutes.

Mix the almonds and egg yolks with a little of the chicken cooking liquid to make a paste. Stir into the casserole about 10 minutes before the end of cooking. Stir in the chopped parsley, then scatter toasted almonds over each serving.

ORANGE SALAD

Try serving this salad with beef slices cooked in sherry (see page 147) or the lamb kidneys (see page 195) for a fresh and light accompaniment.

Serves 4
3 oranges
1 small red onion
2 endive heads
2 tablespoons Moscatel white wine vinegar
4 tablespoons extra virgin olive oil
salt and freshly ground black pepper

Peel the oranges, making sure you remove all the pith and cut out the membrane between the segments.

Peel and slice the onion as thinly as possible. Slice the endive into rounds. Combine the orange segments, onion, and endive. Whisk the juice from the oranges with the vinegar and olive oil and use to dress the salad. Season to taste.

SEVILLE OR BITTER ORANGE SORBET

Seville oranges have such a short season in early January. When available, they are sometimes only used for making marmalade, but their astringency gives a wonderful lift to salads when it is used instead of vinegar.

And here is another use for them: a lively, intensely orange-tasting sorbet. It works well as part of a medley of ices. For example, try teaming it with creamy vanilla and dark chocolate ice creams. If you don't have an ice-cream maker, then stir the mixture every 20 minutes in the freezer until it gets to a desired consistency.

Serves 4
1 cup superfine sugar
1 cup boiling water
1¾ cups Seville orange juice, or other
  sour orange juice mixed with lemon juice
finely grated zest of 1 Seville orange

First, make the sugar syrup. Add the sugar to a measuring jug, pour in the boiling water, and stir vigorously until the sugar has dissolved. This will take less than a minute. You should end up with approx. 1¾ cups of syrup. Set aside to cool completely.

Mix the orange juice, syrup, and zest together and chill in the fridge for an hour or so before churning in your ice-cream maker following the manufacturer's instructions.

MEMBRILLO

Membrillo (Spanish quince paste) and cheese, any cheese, is a fantastic combination. Traditionally, cheeses were made in spring and had to last through the year. By and large, as cheese matures it becomes drier, saltier, and more savory, so the habit grew of eating more mature cheeses with a slab of sweet and sticky membrillo to counteract the dry, grainy texture and salty taste.

While you could buy this copper-colored slab of fruity heaven, it is even better when you have made it yourself: quinces ripen in October, but they last for ages. Set aside an afternoon to make this. This is my mother's recipe, of course.

For every 2 pounds of prepared quince you will need about 3 cups granulated sugar, so scale the quantities up (or down) according to how many quinces you want to use.

2lb quinces, skin on
approx. 3 cups granulated
   sugar

Wash the quinces well and cut out any brown, damaged flesh, then core and cut into cubes.

    Place the quinces and sugar into a large bowl and set aside for 1 hour so that the sugar mixes with the fruit and starts to produce a syrup. Transfer to a large saucepan and place over low heat and keep stirring while the mixture heats up. Once it is cooking, cover with a lid to keep any water from evaporating and to prevent the sugar from burning. Stir every 10 minutes.

    After about 30 minutes, the purée should look sloppy; remove the lid and continue to simmer to reduce the purée to a light syrup. Once all the water has evaporated, the membrillo is ready. This will take about an hour.

    Using a hand blender, purée the liquid until smooth. Put into a suitable jar or container. It will keep in the fridge for up to 6 months.

CHEESE SALAD WITH MEMBRILLO AND WALNUT DRESSING

This recipe works equally well as an appetizer or dessert at a dinner party. The honeyed sweetness of the membrillo complements both the cheese and the bitter winter leaves.

I like to use a mixture of sheep, soft goat, and semi-cured cow cheeses to give a variety of textures and flavors, but you can choose your own favorites.

Serves 4

dressing
1 cup walnuts
5 tablespoons extra virgin
   olive oil
2 tablespoons Moscatel white
   wine vinegar
salt and freshly ground
   black pepper
2oz membrillo, cut into small
   cubes (see page 217)

salad
4oz chicory and radicchio
   salad leaves
2 mint sprigs, leaves stripped
4oz Manchego sheep
   cheese, cut into batons
4oz Mahón cow's cheese,
   cubed
4oz Mont Brut or other soft
   goat cheese, crumbled

Preheat the oven to 425°F.

Break the walnut kernels into largish pieces, and spread them on a baking sheet. Bake in the oven for about 4 to 6 minutes, by which time the nuts will start to color and smell toasty. Remove and let cool. Pick out any debris like skin and small bits of nut.

To make the dressing, whisk the oil and vinegar together, along with a pinch of salt and pepper, then stir in the membrillo cubes and walnuts.

Mix the salad leaves and mint together in a bowl and stir through half the dressing.

Divide the salad between four plates. Arrange the cheeses nicely on top of each portion. Finish off with the rest of the dressing.

CARAMELIZED ALMONDS

These almonds are an addictive snack.

7oz blanched whole almonds
½ cup superfine sugar
¼ cup water

Heat a large frying pan over low to medium heat. Add the ingredients and stir them continuously with a wooden spoon. Be aware that the water will evaporate completely and you might panic because it looks like the recipe is going wrong. Don't worry, though, the sugar will begin to melt and caramelize. This will take about 10 minutes. Don't stop moving the almonds until they are coated in caramel. Remove the almonds from the pan and put them somewhere cold to cool down.

They are ready to eat as they are or with the turrón mousse (see page 225). If you want to eat them as a snack, try scattering a pinch of sea salt over the almonds—it sounds odd, but the sugar-salt combination is delicious.

QUINCE SORBET

I think quinces are too delicious just to be turned into membrillo; their warm, honey flesh makes a delicious sorbet. As with all fruit sorbets, it is important to use ripe, fragrant fruit; just give the quinces a sniff before you buy or pick them. I find that cold-climate quinces—those from the chilly sierras of Spain, or perhaps from your back garden—have more perfume than warm-climate ones grown in North Africa. If you don't have an ice-cream maker, stir the mixture every 20 minutes in the freezer until it reaches the desired consistency.

Serves 4

1½ cups superfine sugar
1½ cups boiling water
1¼lb quinces, peeled, quartered, and cored
juice of 1 lemon

To make the sugar syrup, place the sugar in a measuring jug, pour in the boiling water, and stir well until the sugar has dissolved. This will take less than a minute.

Put the quince pieces and the sugar syrup into a non-stick saucepan. You don't want the mixture to reduce too much, so bring to a boil, cover with a lid, and let the mixture simmer very gently for about 20 minutes, or until the quince is cooked.

Liquidize the quince and syrup while still hot and then strain it; you'll find it easier to do this while the purée is warm. Quince has a slightly grainy texture, so for a smooth effect use a fine strainer—it's a bit of a work-out for the upper arms, but persevere and you'll end up with around 3½ cups of purée.

Add lemon juice to taste: remember that freezing suppresses flavor, so don't be too cautious. Chill the purée in the fridge before churning it in your ice-cream maker, following the manufacturer's instructions.

TURRÓN MOUSSE

This is my colleague Josep Carbonell's recipe—it is a very popular feature on our tapas menu.

There are two basic types of turrón (almond candy): *turrón de Jijona*, or *turrón blando*, which is so soft it is almost like a paste and it sticks rather deliciously to the roof of your mouth; and *turrón de Alicante* or *turrón duro*, which is hard but brittle. For this recipe, make sure that you buy the best quality—*suprema*—soft version, which contains a minimum of 60 percent almonds.

Serves 4

24 golden raisins

4 tablespoons PX sweet
  sherry

2 whole free-range eggs,
  separated

4 tablespoons heavy cream

5oz soft turrón blando

The day before you want to serve the mousse, place the raisins in a bowl with the PX sherry to marinate overnight. The next day, drain the fruit, reserving the sherry.

Use a food processor to blend together the egg yolks, heavy cream, sherry, and turrón. Beat the egg whites until they form stiff peaks, then fold into the turrón mixture.

Put 4 raisins each into the bottom of four wine glasses. Divide the mixture between the glasses and chill for a minimum of 6 hours.

Decorate each glass with two raisins and serve with caramelized almonds (see page 222).

SPANISH WINE

My grandpa Antonio, who ran the bar in Talaván, named his son (my father), Antonio; he in turn named my older brother Antonio, who also named his own son Antonio. My family deserved the nickname "Antoñeque," which has stuck for several generations.

During the heyday of the Antoñeque bar, there were only two others in the village, even though the population was double what it is now; these days there are six. Being a bar owner meant that my grandfather, along with the teachers, doctors, and the mayor, was well respected and had a lot of social standing in the village, and this was a source of pride for all my family.

Grandad's bar was, I suppose, the most upscale of the three thanks to its marble bar top, even though it wasn't what you would call chic. The bar was firmly the domain of the men who chain-smoked, played cards and argued over sports and politics. Women very rarely went there—or indeed to any bar—as respectable women just didn't. If they had to, it was in the company of their father, husband, or brother. And they would never, ever drink alcohol, just sparkling water, known as *gaseosa*.

Back then only the wealthy drank beer. The brand was called Mahou, which was brewed in Madrid, and it used to be collected by donkey from the neighboring village, as that was where the train stopped. Everyone else drank the local wine called *Vino de Pitarra*, which was available on tap.

EXTREMADURAN WINE

Vino de Pitarra is the local name for the white wine that everyone makes for his or her own consumption. It is made wherever there are a few rows of vines, and the word *pitarra* refers to the earthenware vessel in which it was traditionally kept.

Extremadura happens to be the fourth largest producer of grapes in Spain, most of them destined for the production of brandy. So it is no surprise that until recently, Extremadura was not exactly well-known for its quality wines.

All that is changing. Extremadura now has its own *Denominación de Origen* (DO), Ribera del Guadiana, and my friends at Bodegas Las Granadas Coronadas—near the historic town of Trujillo—are a good example of how wine growers are making an enormous effort to improve the local wines, particularly the reds.

SOME SPANISH WINE GRAPE VARIETIES

There are some 65 *Denominación de Origen* (DO) wines scattered throughout Spain and its islands, enough for a whole book. Some, such as Rioja, are famous all over the world, while others are hardly known, even in Spain. The best, I think, are the ones that use indigenous grape varieties. Below are the main ones that you should look out for, along with the DO that they are most commonly associated with, so you know what to look out for on a label.

Albariño

The first time I drank a glass of this white wine it was with hake, and I remember the moment exactly: I thought I'd died and gone to heaven, it was that wonderful! Native to rain-drenched Galicia, it is the most important grape of the Rías Baixas DO. Albariño wine is sometimes very slightly fizzy, a bit like Portugal's *Vinho Verde*. It goes well with any seafood.

Garnacha Tinta

This is the most widely grown red grape in Spain, but its ubiquity doesn't mean a poor-quality grape. The best examples of wine made with Garnacha Tinta come from the Priorat region in Catalonia. The demanding climate, wide planting, slate soils, and low yields, combined with some innovative wine makers, all add up to some stellar wines—with high price tags to match. You will find it blended with another local grape, Cariñena, and, increasingly, international varieties such as Merlot and Cabernet Sauvignon.

Priorat wines aside, Garnacha wines have a raspberry, earthy flavor, and they are easy companions to food. You could drink them with anything from the oxtail stew on page 143 to fried *butifarra* (pork sausages), or grilled vegetables with romesco sauce.

Godello

The name Godello sounds like something from a horror movie, but actually this white grape makes a fruity but crisp, almost mineral-tasting, fresh wine. Native to Galicia, it is important in the Ribeiro and Valdeorras DOs, and it is the region's second most important white wine grape.

Tempranillo

Soft and fruity, Tempranillo is the star of Spanish red wine grapes; it can cope with Spain's climate better than Cabernet Sauvignon, with which it is sometimes blended. I am particularly fond of Tempranillo wine from the Ribera del Duero region, but I'll admit to being biased, as friends of mine own the Cillar de Silos bodega near Burgos in Castilla y León. Their range shows how wonderful this wine is: supple and ripe, while tasting of blackberries and plums.

Tempranillo goes well with all meat and game dishes, especially those to which you have added a dash of hot smoked paprika.

Verdejo

The Verdejo grape makes an aromatic, full-bodied white wine, which experts also describe as herbaceous and even unctuous; it is certainly very drinkable. It is typical of the Rueda DO, which is about two hours' drive northwest from Madrid. Verdejo is a good partner to fish dishes, such as the red mullet, olive, and potato recipe on page 93.

La primera rusa que
tenia honor de pisar
este suelo y tomar una gota
de sol de Andalucia
Malena Samarra

SHERRY

There are wines for different occasions. Sometimes you want something for sharing: the wine has to be drinkable but it is not going to be center stage of the occasion. There may even be a few people who will drink the wine without actually noticing it.

But there are other times when you want to pay attention to your wine, to think about it, to relish its taste and to enjoy how it complements a particular dish. On these occasions there will not be just one sherry that will suit, there will be several. Sherry, in all its styles, is great with food.

You don't have to understand how and why a *flor*—or yeast covering—grows on top of the wine while it's in the barrel, or how the *solera* system (unique to Andalucía) of fractional blending (using wines of varying degrees of barrel age) works. The only thing that matters is that there's some alchemy going on, the results of which enable sherry to partner food in a way that defeats a non-fortified wine. Nibble some Serrano ham with a glass of Fino and then a Sauvignon Blanc, and you'll see what I mean.

There are three main styles:

THE PALE, TANGY, CRISP STYLE

Sherry aficionados can tell the difference between Fino and Manzanilla; I think this takes a bit of practice, but to begin with just remember that Fino and Manzanilla are wines that must be treated like ordinary white wine, i.e., kept in the fridge and drunk within a few days. There are several brands that are widely available, including Tío Pepe, La Gitana and, my favorite, Valdespino's Inocente. This style goes well with any kind of snack, such as olives, nuts, and Serrano ham, as well as with fried seafood, such as the shrimp fritters on page 99.

THE NUTTY, DRY STYLE

Amontillado, Oloroso, and Palo Cortado are made in slightly different ways, so they vary in richness and complexity. But I promise that you will have a very happy time discovering the differences.

Amontillado is an aged and oxidized Fino, so partner it with soups, turkey, rabbit, or mushroom dishes. Richer and smoother than Amontillado, Oloroso sherries are aromatic but still have a clean finish. Palo Cortado, meanwhile, smells like an Amontillado but tastes more like an Oloroso; these days it is often a blend of the two, but actually the real thing is an accident of nature, when a Fino sherry spontaneously oxides.

Oloroso and Palo Cortado work well with game and grilled and roast meats.

THE SWEETIES

All the dry sherries are made using the Palomino grape, but when it comes to sweet sherries, two other grape varieties are used.

Moscatel sherry is made from sun-dried Muscat grapes. Its more famous counterpart is Pedro Ximénez sherry—PX for short—made from the eponymous grape. It looks like molasses and tastes like liquid fruitcake.

Sometimes a little PX is blended with Oloroso to produce a sherry that used to be known as Amoroso; this name has fallen from use, and these days the sherries are referred to as medium or sweet Olorosos. These aren't the same as the export-oriented blended "cream" sherries, such as the famous Harvey's Bristol Cream.

Pale cream sherry is sweetened Fino, while medium sherry is made from Amontillado. You get what you pay for: inexpensive cream sherries will have fructose or grape concentrate blended in, so avoid them.

Moscatel and PX are "end of meal" sherries, which partner squishy mature cheeses, especially blue cheeses, and chocolate desserts. Surprisingly, foie gras, as in the recipe on page 197, goes well with a sweet (*dulce*) Oloroso.

OTHER DRINKS

Drinking habits are very different in Spain and the US. In Spain, people have a drink at any time of day, starting with a swift *aguardiente* (spirit) for breakfast, but getting drunk isn't cool. I think there are different alcohols for different moods, not just different foods.

BEER

I love a beer with tapas, especially when it's really hot outside. Sherry and wine are beautiful with food, but sometimes I want something thirst-quenching with my snacks. Beer goes really well with salty tapas like almonds—or tangy cheeses that have surprisingly large amounts of salt in them.

Perhaps because Spain isn't by tradition a beer-drinking nation, we have slightly different likes and habits than the rest of Europe and the US. For instance, we like big heads on our beers. I enjoy the foam moustache experience—and it was a bit of a surprise to be served a lager for the first time in London, with all the attention given to pouring a beer with no head at all. Widely available Spanish beers include San Miguel and Cruzcampo. If you are heading to Barcelona, look out for micro-breweries such as Glops.

CIDER

In the US, drinking hard cider isn't the most widespread phenomenon, but it is produced and consumed in large quantities in northern Spain, especially Asturias. As a student, one of my pals used to come back from his holidays back home with unlabeled bottles of Asturian cider that we'd all enjoy.

Spanish cider, or *sidra*, is about as boozy as beer—approximately 5 percent alcohol—and it's fizzy thanks to the naturally occurring yeasts; the real thing is never artificially carbonated. In Asturias a cider bar is called a *chigre* (in the rest of Spain it's called simply a *sidrería*) and they take their cider-drinking very seriously.

A trained *escanciador*, or cider-server, will present you with a drink by raising the bottle above his head and then, with much ceremony, pour the cider from about two feet up in the air into a large glass tumbler which he is holding somewhere near his waist—without spilling a drop. It's quite a good party game to try and do yourself. The objective is to make the cider extra bubbly—and then you are expected to drink the cider immediately after pouring. No nursing the glass and sipping it occasionally, or anything restrained like that. Good brands of cider include Gaitero and Fanjul.

Cider is a good alternative to wine with seafood dishes.

SPIRITS

Let's finish with some digestifs.

Anís
Anís, the liquorice-tasting clear spirit beloved by elderly gentlemen as a breakfast digestif all year round, is drunk by the rest of the Spanish population at Christmas time. Perhaps because its core fan base is aging, distilleries have diversified into less alcoholic, flavored versions such as chocolate and hazelnut. Personally, I prefer brandy.

Brandy
There's brandy, and there's Brandy de Jerez; I love its lush smoothness. As the name suggests, Brandy de Jerez is made by the sherry

bodegas in and around Jerez de la Frontera in Andalucía. Like all the other types of brandy, it is distilled from fermented grape juice or crushed—but not pressed—grape pulp and skin. Nearly all Brandy de Jerez is made from distillate produced elsewhere in Spain, mostly in La Mancha and Extremadura, as the local Palomino grapes are used in the production of sherry.

Unlike all other brandies, the resulting spirit is aged in the *solera* system (the same as in sherry production), which gives the alcohol its brandy color, imbues it with floral, fruity, slightly sweet flavors, and soothes its firewater nature.

Since the sherry bodegas all commission their own distillate, and then put it into casks which previously have had different kinds of sherry in them, the resulting brandies are by no means uniform in flavor. But they are all wonderful! I suggest you start by sampling those from Fernando de Castilla, González Byass, Osborne, and Sánchez Romate.

Also look out for Penedès brandy from Catalonia. There are two local producers, Torres and Mascaro. The brandy uses local grapes and French oak casks. It is more robust than French Cognac, and drier than Brandy de Jerez. It's good hearty stuff.

SPANISH FOOD AND WINE SOURCES

You've bought the book, you like the recipes, so now you need the ingredients. Supermarkets everywhere are increasingly stocking Spanish products but for something special, try the following shops:

ONLINE

La Tienda
www.tienda.com
Telephone: (800) 710-4304
3601 La Grange Parkway
Toano, VA 23168

Delicas de España
www.deliciasdeespana.com
Telephone: (305) 669-4485
4016 SW 57th Avenue
Miami, FL 33155

Amigo Foods
www.amigofoods.com
Telephone: (800) 627-2544
350 NE 75th Street
Miami, FL 33138

igourmet
www.igourmet.com/spanishfood.asp
Telephone: (877) 446-8763
508 Delaware Avenue
West Pittston, PA 18463

SPECIALITY FOOD SHOPS

Brindisa
Floral Hall, Stoney Street, Borough Market,
London SE1
Telephone: 0044 20 7407 1036
www.brindisa.com
Brindisa are the pioneers of importing Spanish food to the UK, and have a great range of high quality foodstuffs, from salted almonds to fresh chorizo. You can visit their shops in London, or call them to see which stockists they supply.

Despana
www.despananyc.com
Telephone: (212) 219-5050
408 Broome Street
New York, NY 10013
A Spanish boutique located between Soho and Little Italy that specializes in offering quality gourmet food products produced exclusively in Spain.

Deli-Iberico
www.cafeiberico.com/deli
Telephone: (312) 573-1510
739 LaSalle Drive
Chicago, IL 60610
A tapas restaurant and delicatessen located in Chicago. Offers deli trays, special sausages and hams, packaged foods, oils and vinegars, and a variety of paella pans and pottery.

The Spanish Table
www.spanishtable.com
Telephone: (206) 682-2827
1426 Western Avenue
Seattle, WA 98101
The Spanish Table offers food and cookware
from Spain, Portugal, and beyond. They also
have stores in Berkeley and Mill Valley, CA and
Sante Fe, NM.

La Española Meats, Inc.
www.laespanolameats.com
Telephone: (310) 539-0455
25020 Doble Avenue
Harbor City, California 90710
La Española is an importer, distributor, retailer,
and wholesaler of fine Spanish foods. They also
manufacture premium Spanish-style sausages
and cured meat products.

SHERRY SUPPLIERS

Snooth, Inc.
www.snooth.com/wines/sherry
162 Madison Avenue, Floor 4
New York, NY 10016

Wine Chateau
www.winechateau.com
Telephone: (800) 946-3190
160 Durham Avenue
Metuchen, NJ 08840

The Wine Buyer
www.thewinebuyer.com
Telephone: (800) 946-3937
1950 Route 23
Wayne, NJ 07470

CONVERSION CHARTS

Oven temperatures

Celsius	Fahrenheit	Gas Mark	Description
110 C	225 F	¼	cool
130 C	250 F	½	cool
140 C	275 F	1	very low
150 C	300 F	2	very low
170 C	325 F	3	very low
180 C	350 F	4	moderate
190 C	375 F	5	moderate / hot
200 C	400 F	6	hot
220 C	425 F	7	hot
230 C	450 F	8	very hot

Weight: metric to imperial

10 g	0.25 oz
15 g	0.25 oz
25 g	1 oz
50 g	1.75 oz
75 g	2.75 oz
100 g	3.5 oz
150 g	5.5 oz
175 g	6 oz
200 g	7 oz
225 g	8 oz
250 g	9 oz
275 g	9.75 oz
300 g	10.5 oz
350 g	12 oz
375 g	13 oz
400 g	14 oz
425 g	15 oz
450 g	1 lb
500 g	1 lb 2 oz
700 g	1.5 lb
750 g	1 lb 10 oz
1 kg	2.25 lb
1.25 kg	2 lb 12 oz
1.5 kg	3 lb 5 oz
2 kg	4.5 lb
2.25 kg	5 lb
2.5 kg	5.5 lb

Liquids: metric to imperial

1.25 ml	0.25 teaspoon	
2.5 ml	0.5 teaspoon	
5 ml	1 teaspoon	
15 ml	1 tablespoon	
30 ml	1 fl oz	
50 ml	2 fl oz	
100 ml	3.5 fl oz	
150 ml	5 fl oz	0.25 pint
200 ml	7 fl oz	0.33 pint
300 ml	10 fl oz	0.5 pint
500 ml	18 fl oz	
600 ml	20 fl oz	1 pint
700 ml		1.25 pints
850 ml		1.5 pints
1 liter		1.75 pints
1.2 liters		2 pints

Length: metric to imperial

5 mm	0.25 inch
1 cm	0.5 inch
2 cm	0.75 inch
3 cm	1.25 inch
4 cm	1.5 inch
5 cm	2 inch
6 cm	2.5 inch
7 cm	2.75 inch
8 cm	3.25 inch
9 cm	3.5 inches
10 cm	4 inches
30cm	1 foot

INDEX

ACKNOWLEDGMENTS

Firstly, I'd like to thank Vicky Bennison for all her hard work and patience.

I'd like to thank my sister Isabel, my brother Antonio and my sister-in-law Maria José, my nephews Juan and Antonio, and my nieces Carmen, Marina and Cristina for their support and inspiration.

All the Kyle Cathie team, especially Kyle Cathie for her confidence in me, and Sophie Allen the editor; Martine Carter my agent; Emma Lee the photographer; Annie Nichols the food stylist; Tabitha Hawkins, the props stylist; and the design team at Two Associates.

The Spanish Ambassador in London, H.E. Mr. Carles Casajuana.

Monika Linton, for opening my eyes to good-quality Spanish products in England.

Julio Reoyo, Imma Redondo, and David Eyre – my mentors. José Andrés, Elena Arzak, Angela Hartnett and Mark Hix for their support.

A special thanks to my friends Germán Arroyo, Fernando Lanzas and Jorge Postigo for their support.

Everyone at the Brindisa restaurants, especially Esperanza Añonuevo and Josep Carbonell for their great recipes and patience. Also, Angel Alonso, Ratnesh Bagdai, Victor Calvente, Camilo Corredor, Alex Fletcher, Miguel García, Paul Grout, Joel Placeres and Rubén Maza. The Brindisa team in Balham, especially Abi Lawley, Cristina Pasantes, James Robinson, Claire Roff and Rudolf von Vollmar. The Brindisa team at the Borough Market shop, especially Jackie Crank and Rosmary Valdes.

The various representatives of Spanish institutions in London: The Extremadura UK Trade Office, especially the lovely Olga Salazar, for her incredible work promoting our region; the people at the Spanish Tourist Office, especially Ignacio Vasallo and Ana María Bermúdez. The teams of ICEX, the cultural office at the Spanish Embassy, Excal and The Sherry Institute in London.

The many wineries in Spain including: Cillar de Silos, especially Oscar Aragón and his family; Bodega Alvear, especially María Alvear; Bodega Las Granadas Coronadas; Bodega José Estévez, especially María Isabel Estévez; Bodega Emilio Hidalgo, especially Fernando M. Hidalgo; Bodega González Byass. Other producers and promoters in Spain. P.D.O. 'Dehesa de Extremadura', especially Álvaro Rivas; P.D.O. 'Pimentón de la Vera', especially Bonifacio Sánchez.; the Roa brothers of Jamones Roa; Jose María Hernández, producer of pimentón de La Vera 'La Dalia'; cheesemakers Mario Blasco Queserías del Casar, and Fernando Fregeneda of La Antigua Zamorano cheese; Patricio Aparicio of El Trillo pulses.

All the people at London's Borough Market with a big thanks to The Wild Mushroom Company, especially Tony Booth and John Leavey, Wyndham House Poultry Co and The Ginger Pig. All the people in the Boqueria Market in Barcelona.

Thanks to Elsa Toro for our 38 years of friendship; Diego Elso, for our walks in the mountains looking for mushrooms. Jo Aherne, Amelia Aragón, Tim Atkin, Richard Bigg, Beatriz Blázquez, Bea Pascual, my Tortilla Club friends. Thomas Aagard, Natali and Victoria Agenjo, Cathie Arrington, Nieves Barragán, Rafael Chicano, María Cobo, Eduardo de Felipe, Jonathan Jeffery, Dioni Jiménez, Ian Galletly, Consoli and Sonia García, Venice Gainfort-Head, Billy Macqueen, Ascen Martín, Juan Antonio Mariscal Burgos, Isabel Montes de Oca, Ana Rosa Moreno, Anabel Toribio, Celia Resel, Marianne Rodríguez, Enric Rovira, Tom and Rebecca Pincus and Jose Daniel Valero.

And the rest of my friends and family.

Published in 2010 by Kyle Books, an imprint of
Kyle Cathie Ltd.
www.kylebooks.com

Distributed by National Book Network
4501 Forbes Blvd., Suite 200
Lanham, MD 20706
Phone: (800) 462-6420

First published in Great Britain in 2009 by
Kyle Cathie Limited
www.kylecathie.com

ISBN: 978-1-906868-09-3

A cataloging-in-publication record for this title is available from the Library of Congress

10 9 8 7 6 5 4 3 2 1

Design: Two Associates
Photography: Emma Lee
Project editor: Sophie Allen
Food stylists: Annie Nichols and José Pizarro
Props stylist: Tabitha Hawkins
Copy editor: Emily Hatchwell
Proofreader: Stephanie Evans
Production: Gemma John

Color reproduction by Sang Choy International
Printed and bound in China

BANDEJA DE GAMBAS 48€